ANTIQUE NEEDLEWORK TOOLS

and Embroideries

MORNING DRESS.

Engraven for the Thirty Second Number of New Series of La Belle Assemblée, June 1, 1812.
Printed for John Bell, Southampton Street Strand.

A Lady Embroidering – fashion plate for 'Morning Dress'. From La Belle Assemblée, June 1812.

Opposite: Spanish walnut (see Colour Plate 138, page 125).

ANTIQUE NEEDLEWORK TOOLS
and Embroideries

Nerylla Taunton

Antique Collectors' Club

ISBN 1 85149 253 4

British Library Cataloguing-in-Publication Data
A catalogue record for this book is available from the British Library

Printed in England
by the Antique Collectors' Club Ltd., Woodbridge, Suffolk
on Consort Royal Era Satin paper
supplied by the Donside Paper Company, Aberdeen, Scotland

Contents

Bonbonnière box (see Colour Plate 191, page 177).

Preface and Acknowledgements

My interest in antique needlework tools began when my Mother gave me my Grandmother's silver thimble. I was then in my teens and that silver thimble sparked an interest in collecting thimbles that quickly expanded to include all needlework tools.

My greatest frustration during those early years was the lack of information about needlework tools and the publication of *The History of Needlework Tools and Accessories* by Sylvia Groves opened up a new vista. This wonderful book has been my inspiration and constant companion and one of my greatest regrets is that I never had the opportunity to meet Sylvia Groves before she died.

The sharing of knowledge amongst collectors is fundamental to the greater understanding of any subject. In my early days of collecting I was fortunate to meet the Australian collectors – Heather Joynes, Wendy Ritchie and Iris Woolley and over the years we have spent many invaluable hours viewing and discussing the many aspects of our collecting interest.

My interest in needlework tools and associated embroideries developed to such an extent that in the 1970s I opened an antique shop in Sydney, Australia specialising in these fields. I am a member of the Australian Antique Dealers Association and a Valuer for the Department of the Arts. It is interesting that after twenty years of being in business my fascination with my speciality has never waned but rather has overwhelmingly increased.

In the early days of my business Deirdre Stokes liaised for me in England with my buying. Those were the days when Sheila Smith had her wonderful shop of treasures in Queen Street, Bath that is sadly missed and she, Elena Innocenti and Cynthia Leavens had an endless supply of needlework tools, the likes of which are not readily available today. The time I spent visiting Sheila and Cynthia and discussing needlework tools has been invaluable and is not forgotten. This was also the time that Bridget McConnel started the Thimble Society of London and Thimble Collectors International was formed in the U.S.A.

In the early 1980s I attended my first Convention in Philadelphia organised by T.C.I. and it was then that I was fortunate to meet in person Christina Bertrand, Ann Blakeslee, Dickey Everson, Edwin Holmes, Jo Anne Rath, Gay Ann Rogers and numerous other knowledgeable collectors that I had previously only known through correspondence.

As the years progressed I have been fortunate to be able to visit collectors all around the world, view their collections and have in-depth discussions about the various items. This has included the collections of Christina Bertrand, Dickey Everson, Edwin Holmes, Estelle Horowitz, Ruth Mann, Min Maude, Molly Pearce,

Di Pelham Burn, Phyllis Underhill, Elizabeth Waciorski and numerous others who have granted me time and hospitality to expand my knowledge.

In the mid 1980s Elaine Gaussen put an enormous amount of work into forming the Dorset Thimble Society and Elaine's leadership has been ably followed by Jean Scott and Joan Roberts and the Conventions organised by this Society have greatly expanded the knowledge of collectors.

The Needlework Tool Collectors Society of Australia, based in Melbourne, was formed in 1987 by Katrina and Jenny Cowen. This Society has been invaluable in Australia and meetings are held regularly in most capital cities and a bi-annual Convention held. This has been tremendously successful in increasing the knowledge and horizons of collectors that are more remote from other parts of the world.

In England I have been especially helped by Sonia and Nick Cordell, Min and Richard Maude and Elizabeth and Janusz Waciorski. They have opened their homes to Colvin and me and given freely of their time and been true friends to us both, over many years. Joan and Don Harrison and their daughter Rae have been greatly respected in the English lace-making world and Don's death meant that not only did I lose a dear friend but someone whose knowledge of lace bobbins I greatly respected. To lose Barbara Todd was not only to lose a close friend but the loss of one of the most intuitive antique dealers that I have ever known. Our memories of the time we spent with her both in Whitby and when she stayed with us in Australia, will not be forgotten. I would also like to thank Catherine Alder, Jean Burnett, John Cowen, Erna Hiscock, Pamela Hudson, Brenda Page, Dory Paton, Judith Pollitt, Enid Riley, Lois and Ken Sawyer, Barbara Springall, Chris Vernon and Rosemary Waller for their help over many years and to many others who have helped me by finding that elusive needlework tool or scrap of information.

In Australia, Anne Baker's teaching has added tremendously to my knowledge of embroidery and its history. I have also been very fortunate to have many specific questions answered in my correspondence with Margaret Swain in Edinburgh and the time I have spent in Witney, England, with Kathleen Scaramanga discussing samplers and seventeenth and eighteenth embroidery has been invaluable.

Over the years various museums, art galleries and libraries have been a great help to me with my research. These include The British Museum Library (London and Colindale); The Guildhall Library, London and The National Gallery, London. I would like to especially thank Joanne Charlton (The Wallace Collection, London), Frances Bowers (The Whitworth Art Gallery, Manchester), Annette Hamilton (Librarian, The Embroiderers' Guild NSW Inc.) and Nicole Tetzner (Windsor Castle Library).

Writing for various publications has been something that I have always enjoyed and the rapport I have had with various editors has been tremendous. Since 1983 I have contributed a regular feature article to *Antiques in New South Wales* and the Editor and owner André Jaku has been incredibly supportive to me. My association with Express Publications began ten years ago with the introduction of their magazine *Australian Country Craft and Decorating* and I have been a feature writer for this publication. I now write a regular feature article for *Embroidery and Cross Stitch* - a more recent Express Publications venture and it is a pleasure to work with and have the co-operation of the editors - Sue Aiken, Robyn Wilson and Sue Stravs and their photographer Tim Connolly.

I was invited to be a speaker at the 1989 Dorset Thimble Society Convention in England and in 1990 at the T.C.I. Convention in Louisville, Kentucky, U.S.A. The photography for these slide programmes was undertaken by Scott Donkin in Sydney and received rave reviews. Since the early 1980s Scott has regularly undertaken photographic projects for me - some of which have not been easy as anyone who has experienced photographing small silver items will know. Consequently, there was no debate in my mind as to who would undertake the photography for this book. Completing these photographs took numerous sessions at Scott's studio and it was an absolute delight to work so harmoniously with him. The results of his work are exceptional and I am most grateful for the extra time and care Scott put into this task. Unless otherwise acknowledged all the photographs are Scott's work. The sketches in this book were undertaken by my son, Steven Taunton.

For many years I have visited The Antique Collectors' Club in Woodbridge, England, negotiating with Diana Steel for the publication of *Chatelaines - Utility to Glorious Extravagance* that I co-authored. Over those years I have come to know and admire Diana Steel and without a doubt feel that she heads the foremost publishing house specialising in books relating to the world of antiques. I am delighted that Diana Steel agreed to publish this book and am most grateful for her enthusiasm and encouragement.

Special thanks are due to my editor Peter Robertson for all his help in the preparation of this book and to Lynn Taylor for the exceptional work that she has put into the book's design. The cover was chosen by Diana Steel and photographed by Tim Ferguson. I am also most grateful to Pamela Clabburn for contributing the Foreword.

Through all the various ventures I have undertaken, the greatest support I have received has come from my husband, Colvin who has always been there to give me encouragement. He, together with Steven and Joanne, has always had a belief in my ability to achieve my goals and it is thanks to my family that I have had the confidence to fulfil the ventures I have undertaken.

French egg-shaped container for miniature sewing tools (see Colour Plate 145, page 131).

Foreword

*A*ny tool which is well made and completely functional has a beauty of its own, whether it be a spade, screwdriver or saucepan, but few trades combine tools of utility and beauty as effortlessly as that of needlework. Imagine life without scissors, needles or pins. They are as vital to everyday living as any other basic tool and they are as old as Adam and Eve. Is it any wonder that over the ages with much use and refining they have acquired a beauty and a 'right feel' that gives an intense pleasure to the user.

Needlework has always been a business for some and a pastime for others and thus has encompassed both rich and poor. Great ladies, queens and princesses all sewed; in their cases generally embroidery or possibly church vestments. The sewing exploits of Mary, Queen of Scots and Bess of Hardwick in the sixteenth century are well documented and there were many others like them. The less well-to-do and the merely genteel combined embroidery with the making of dress accessories, if not the dresses themselves. Ladies' maids, and there were many of them, earned their living sewing for their mistresses, altering dresses, stitching exquisite underwear and repairing both clothes and household linen. The standard of darning and mending was very high indeed in the past. The poor at the bottom of the pile slaved with their needles, working in poor light and unhealthy conditions, sewing every type of work which could be sold in the shops. Thus every class would need a range of implements from those made of precious metals to those of wood or tin, plainly shaped and undecorated.

The wonder really is that up to about thirty years ago no one had bothered to research the origins of needlework tools. Perhaps they seemed so ordinary and were made and sold in such thousands that they did not appear interesting to most people – they were just there. Then Sylvia Groves fired many peoples' interest with her book *The History of Needlework Tools* which describes them all and gives a real insight into their usage and which opened many eyes, including, as she says, Nerylla's, and, I may add, mine.

However, since then more research has been done and it was time for a bigger and more up-to-date book to appear, especially one which covers three continents. It is so easy to become far too parochial and not realise that other parts of the world have different versions of everyday items.

This book, adorned with really superb photographs, describes it all and gives a real insight into the tools used through three centuries. It also touches on some of the embroideries which the right tools helped to make so perfect.

It is a 'must' for collectors and will help to identify those objects in their possession and show how some of the more unusual were used. We should all be grateful to Nerylla for enlightening us.

Pamela Clabburn

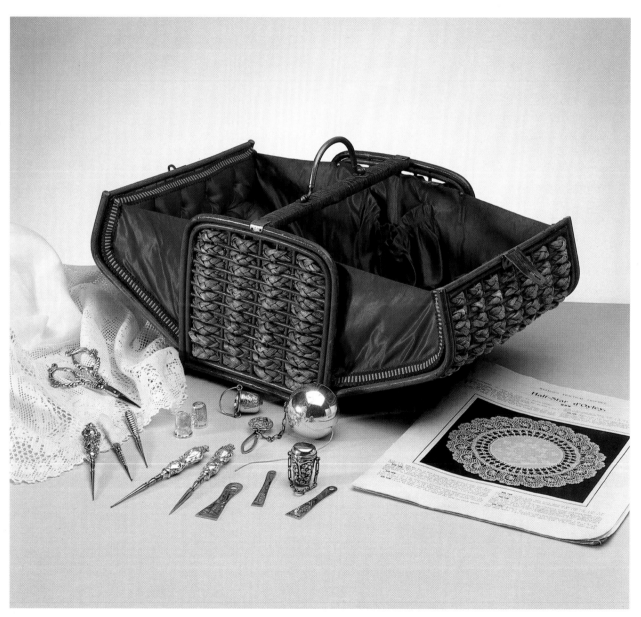

An Edwardian lady's sewing basket, crochet and pattern book and her typical Edwardian sterling silver needlework tools (see Colour Plate 216, page 198).

Introduction

The history of needlework tools and their use in the creation of embroidery, has been one of my major interests for the greater part of my life. During the past twenty years, as an antique dealer, I have tried to pass on to collectors the knowledge I have learnt from my research. This has been in the form of information sheets, lectures, articles or more importantly, verbal explanations to collectors who have visited my shop.

The time now seems appropriate for me to put this information into a book in the same way as I would explain, face to face, any aspect of needlework tools to an interested collector.

Twenty years of answering collectors' questions and queries have given me a knowledge of what they find confusing and what aspects are of most interest or need clarifying. I have also found that collectors are most interested in needlework tools being slotted into periods of time and they like to relate them to the social scene at the time and the hand-work that was in fashion.

As a general guide, English needlework tools readily available for collectors fit into three definite periods of time. The ivory tools of the Georgian era, the mother-of-pearl tools that are synonymous with the Victorian era and the sterling silver tools that are typically Edwardian. Of course there are numerous exceptions to this broad definition but as a general guide it is helpful to collectors. There has always been an overlapping of styles. No one imagines that craftsmen ceased producing Georgian and Regency style articles immediately Victoria was crowned, but rather, a gradual change of style developed. This makes it impossible to give a definite date for most needlework tools and they can only be slotted into an appropriate era.

While ivory tools with restrained lines were at their peak of popularity in England, a different situation was occurring in France. The Dieppe area was producing glorious carved ivory needlework tools at the same time as exquisite mother-of-pearl tools were being sold in Paris at the Palais Royal. There is no doubt that both these varieties of French needlework tools are amongst the finest ever produced.

Hand-made pincushions and needlebooks give us a glimpse into the lives of eighteenth and nineteenth century ladies and the fascination in collecting these items is not only that of the items themselves but with the scenes that we imagine surrounding them.

Every book written on any particular subject adds a link to the chain of knowledge about that subject. Hopefully, I have been able to add my link and future generations will study and treasure these fascinating collectables.

Colour Plate 4. Stumpwork 'Cabbinet' embroidered by Hannah Smith. The important letter written by Hannah in 1657 and left in this casket, fully documents that she was almost twelve years old when she completed the embroidered panels and the casket was made up in London in 1656. 12 x 7 x 10in. (30.5 x 17.75 x 25.5cm.) Courtesy: The Whitworth Art Gallery, University of Manchester.

Colour Plate 1. Opposite. Silver Bodkins incorporating an ear-spoon. James I c.1615. The scratched decoration is typical for this era. English. Length of longest 5¼in. (14.6cm.)

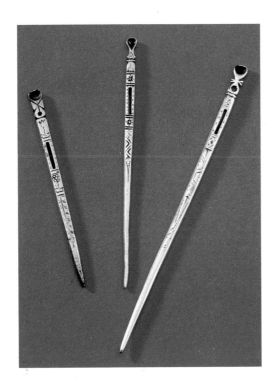

Chapter One
The Seventeenth Century

Ever since early man fashioned primitive garments there has been a need for some type of needlework tool. A sharp pointed implement, which would have been the forerunner of the stiletto and similar to an awl, must have been used to make holes so that the edges of a garment could be laced together. No doubt an implement was gradually developed that could be used to thread fibres through these holes and consequently a bodkin was born. A needle would have been a natural development incorporating the two functions of a stiletto and bodkin and a natural progression would have been to protect the finger with some form of 'pusher' which eventually became the thimble as we know it today.

The earliest needlework implements available today for collectors, apart from thimbles, date from early in the seventeenth century. At this period of time silver bodkins were used for threading cord, ribbon or lace. These bodkins, with a 'scratched' decoration are sometimes initialled and occasionally dated. Ear-spoons, considered a necessity, are frequently found at one end of these bodkins. Rare examples have a maker's mark and Sir Charles Jackson in his research has dated one example with the mark 'MH Conjoined' as 1613. Bodkins from the period of James I (Colour Plate 1) are quite large, measuring from five inches (12.7 cm.) to just over seven inches (17.8 cm.) in length.

To fully appreciate the style of needlework implements dating from the last half of the seventeenth century it is important to picture the aesthetic tastes of that time. It was the age of oak – rooms were panelled and had heavy beams. Furniture such as oak joined chairs, court cupboards and refectory tables were

Colour Plate 2. Raised embroidery (now known as Stumpwork). The figures, pears and dog have been heavily padded and the camel worked entirely of beads. c.1660. 14½ x 9¾in. (36.8 x 24.8cm.)

deeply carved. Fabrics were an important ingredient, whether made by the housewife or the professional hand. Inventories are full of references to cushions, screens, wall hangings and bed coverings and a visit to a furnished manor house in England allows one to set the scene. Against this background it is not at all strange that a heavy form of embroidery was also popular.

This heavy padded raised embroidery is now known as stumpwork, a name that does not appear to have been used before the reference in *Old English Embroidery* by Frances and Hugh Marshall published in 1894. This distinctive embroidery was worked on heavy white satin that had previously been stamped with a pattern – a possible origin of the name stumpwork coming from 'embroidery worked on the stamp'. Further support for this argument is found in the 1882 publication of *The Dictionary of Needlework* by Caulfeild & Saward where they refer to raised embroidery as 'Embroidery on the Stamp'. Because of the repetitiveness of designs seen on surviving pieces of stumpwork it is quite likely that the requirements for this form of needlework were sold in a kit form similar to those of the late twentieth century.

Caskets, mirror surrounds and pictures (Colour Plate 2) were embroidered in this distinctive seventeenth century heavy padded style. A small box (Colour Plate 3) although not as grand as the numerous caskets that have survived, does clearly show the heavy raised style of embroidery and the use of sequins and metal thread. There is an interesting label on the base of this box :-

ON LOAN FROM
Sir G. Ducket, August 1899.

Colour Plate 3. Small Stumpwork box with raised leaves and flowers fitted with wire hinges and metal press-catch. Overall decoration of metal thread and sequins. c.1660.
4 x 2¾ x 2¼in. (10.2 x 7 x 5.8cm.)

Numerous prestigious exhibitions of early embroideries were held at the end of the nineteenth and early twentieth century and no doubt this small box was included in one of those exhibitions. It is also no coincidence that this was the time when interest in seventeenth century embroideries was at its peak and prices realised in sales were relatively far in excess of prices today.

In complete contrast to this small box is the wonderful and well documented 'cabbinet' made by Hannah Smith (Colour Plate 4, see page 14) and now housed at The Whitworth Art Gallery, University of Manchester, England. This casket is important because as well as being a fine example, it contained the following letter written by Hannah Smith that shows us how young she was when she undertook such an enormous task as well as giving us an accurate dating for stumpwork:-

> 'The yere of our Lord being 1657:
> if ever I have any thoughts about the time; when I went to Oxford; as it may be I may; when I have forgoten the time; to fortifi my self; I may loock in this paper & find it; I went to Oxford; in the yere of 1654; & my being thare; near 2 yers; for I went in 1654; & I stayed there; 1655 & I cam away; in 1656; & I was allmost 12 yers; of age; when I went; & I mad an end of my cabbinete; at Oxford; & my ? & my cabbinet; was mad up; in the yere of 1656 at London; I have ritten this; to fortiffi my self; & thos that shall inquir; about it.   Hannah Smith'

Because most pieces of seventeenth century embroidery have been exposed to sunlight for a considerable period of time, their colours have faded and dulled. It is only when one views unfinished pieces that have not been exposed to light, that one becomes aware of the vibrancy of the colours that were used for stumpwork embroidery. These vivid colours can be seen in the incomplete embroidery 'The Sacrifice of Isaac' (Colour Plate 5). The embroidery shows the two young men left with the ass while Abraham takes the wood, builds an altar with it, and places his young son Isaac upon the altar. As Abraham takes the knife to slay his son the angel of the Lord stops him (seen in the cloud above his head) and provides a ram (which is caught in a thicket by his horns) to be used as a sacrifice instead of Isaac. This incomplete embroidery also clearly shows the black outline of the pattern, and this patterning on other unworked pieces the author has viewed is almost identical, enforcing the view that the satin was sold with the picture already outlined.

Colour Plate 5. Unfinished Stumpwork embroidery - 'The Sacrifice of Isaac'. Incomplete embroideries not exposed to daylight are important as they show the vibrancy of the coloured silks used during the 17th century. The outline of the unworked pattern is clearly shown. c.1660. 13½ x 10in. (34.4 x 25.4cm.)

Colour Plate 6. Below. Silver thimble - Royal Marriage Commemorative - 1662. This thimble is decorated with profiles of Charles II and Catherine of Braganza. The thimble is marked 'G' (the maker's mark) and inscribed around the rim with the owner's initials 'AK'.

This heavy decorative style, so popular in the seventeenth century, is reflected in the needlework tools of the day. Silver thimbles were heavy and quite distinctive with an early example, that is possibly one of the first made to commemorate a Royal event, decorated with oval profile medallions of Charles II and Catherine of Braganza (Colour Plate 6). Catherine landed at Portsmouth in May, 1662 and although suffering from a cold and fever made a favourable impression on Charles, the wedding taking place soon after. Examples of this important thimble are to be seen at the British Museum and the Museum of London and also in at least three private collections. It is interesting to note that the thimbles available for examination were not all made by the same maker – the illustrated example has a maker's mark 'G' and is inscribed around the rim with the owner's initials 'AK'. This thimble, found by an excavator during November, 1991 near Brandon Parva, Norfolk, is in excellent condition and has been well authenticated.

Sylvia Groves, in her excellent book, illustrates and describes a small brocade casket that was used by a child during the seventeenth century to hold personal possessions including needlework tools. Eric Delieb also writes about a similar 'book-shaped' container with padded domed covers, the centre containing a thimble, needle pad, notebook and mirror. A scissors' case containing fine steel scissors was mounted on the back of the cover. The dating given for this 'article' is c.1640.

The delightful child's sewing compendium illustrated in Colour Plates 7 & 8 is very similar to those described by Groves and Delieb. Its rectangular shape has been covered with red and silver silk brocade, one side domed with a padded pincushion. The other side has been fitted with a scissors' case that holds a pair of steel scissors (of a later date). When opened, one side of the 'book' has been made with a recess to hold a seventeenth century child's thimble. This rare silver thimble, in excellent condition, has a frieze of two hearts flanked by cherubs and leaves. The compendium, which has been wonderfully preserved, also contains a notebook with a dry-point writing implement, a mirrored compartment and a purse. The two halves are hinged and are held closed with a silver catch.

It is particularly interesting that the author has viewed another compendium (not as well preserved) made from seemingly identical silk brocade with similar fittings and silver mounts. It would appear that these extremely rare seventeenth century treasures were made professionally rather than by ladies in their homes. Dry-point writing implements were, by the end of the seventeenth century, completely out of vogue as, by this time, graphite pencils were in general use. Any child that owned such an expensive case would have belonged to a wealthy family and would have used the most up to date writing implement.

Colour Plate 7. 17th century child's sewing compendium covered with red and silver silk brocade. A pair of scissors fits into the padded scabbard-shaped holder on one side, the other side is domed and padded to form a pincushion. A silver catch at the front enables the compendium to be closed. 2¼ x 1¾ x 1½in. (5.8 x 4.5 x 3.9cm.) Private Collector.

Colour Plate 8. Interior of the 17th century child's sewing compendium showing a purse, mirrored compartment, notebook with dry-point writing implement and the recess in the padded domed side to hold a thimble. A wonderful contemporary silver thimble, with a frieze of two hearts flanked by cherubs and leaves, is also shown and this thimble fits perfectly into the recess. Private Collector.

Colour Plate 9. Sampler worked by EH and dated 1669. Rows of padded embroidery including Tudor roses and boxers are followed by the alphabet and the following message:-

'Let Titel be the name of Truth
This is the practis of my youth
With care and cost this have I wrought
And finished with a virgin thought'

Size: 20 x 10in. (51 x 25.5cm.)

Colour Plate 10. Silver and velvet pin-ball with contemporary chain. The circular silver frame has a vandyke edging and the original blue velvet still retains some of its pile. c.1680. English. Diameter 2½in. (6.4cm.)

Colour Plate 11. Silver combination thimble/ needlecases with typical scratch-engraved decoration. Each example has a steel spring-catch and a three-lugged hinge. c.1660 - 1680. English. Length 3½in. (9cm.)

Embroidering a sampler was another important achievement in the life of a young girl and although not as heavy as stumpwork, the sampler (Colour Plate 9) does have Tudor roses and boxers embroidered in a much heavier manner than samplers a century later. This sampler, initialled EH and dated 1669, is typical of band samplers worked during this period. The linen used was woven in narrow widths – hence the use of the word band – and frequently samplers from this era were twice as long as the illustrated example.

Samuel Pepys, who is well known for the diary he wrote during the 1660s, gives us a wonderful insight into the lifestyles of all levels of society at that time. What is not so well known is that Pepys kept a number of London Tradesmen's cards that date from early in the 1660s until the 1690s, and these have been preserved in the British Museum with an interesting text by Sir Ambrose Heal. Sir Ambrose talks about the perspicacity of Pepys in collecting these Trade Cards and although none refer to thimbles or scissors, the Trade Card of Francis Dodsworth says he '...maketh & seleth all sorts o Gold Silver, & Silk Laces, & Fringes, Gold & Silver Thred of all sorts...' There are quite a few Trade Cards in this collection advertising the wares of Mercers and Haberdashers and Pepys may have been influenced by his childhood as the son of a tailor. These are the Tradesmen who would have supplied ladies with their embroidery requisites.

Thimbles were not the only needlework implement to follow the heavy decorative style of the seventeenth century. There is a striking resemblance about the silver thimble/needlecases, pin-balls and scissors' cases, all with their scratch-engraved decoration, that matches the heavy furnishings that were in vogue at that period of time. Although rare, occasionally seventeenth century needlework tools do come onto the market and the pin-ball (Colour Plate 10) is such an example. This pin-ball has a circular silver frame with a vandyke edging and the original blue velvet still retains some of its pile. Sir Charles Jackson has dated a similar example with the maker's mark, IA with a crown above, to c.1680-85.

Silver needlecases with a compartment for a thimble are quite distinctive. They are scratch-engraved (Colour Plate 11) and each end opens with a steel spring-catch and a three-lugged hinge. These thimble/needlecases appear to be earlier than the pin-balls and date from 1660-1680.

Silver scissors' cases from the last half of the seventeenth century again have the distinctive scratch-engraved decoration and three-lugged hinge. It is rare to find

Colour Plate 12. Three very rare matching 17th century silver needlework tools joined by contemporary chains to a central ring - now called a chatelaine. The pin-ball, combination thimble/needlecase (initialled "MB') and scissors' case all have matching scratch engraved decoration. The scissors, that appear to be original, are steel with heavy silver handles. The silver thimble is a replacement but is from the same period of time. English. c.1680. Length 8in. (20.3cm.)

scissors' cases with original scissors but the cases on their own are very collectable.

To find three matching needlework tools from the seventeenth century is extremely rare and the examples in Colour Plate 12 form the only set the author has been able to locate. The pin-ball, scissors' case and combination thimble/needlecase are made of silver with matching scratch-engraved decoration and are typical of the heavy style of implements so much in favour in that era. The chains are of a comparable age and these needlework tools may have been worn attached to the waist band individually or as a set, this being the safest place to keep such precious possessions. This set of needlework tools would not have been called a chatelaine as this word was not used to describe a waist-hung fashion accessory until 1828 (see *Chatelaines – Utility to Glorious Extravagance*). The thimble/needlecase and the scissors' case in this set open with a steel spring-catch and both have a three-lugged hinge. The pin-ball has replacement fabric which is acceptable as it is rare to find the original fabric still intact, as in the case of the pin-ball previously discussed. The thimble/needlecase is engraved with the initials 'M.B'. The scissors' case holds a pair of steel scissors with heavy silver handles which appear to be original as they fit perfectly into the case and are from the same period of time. The thimble shown in the same colour plate was not originally with this set, but is contemporary and therefore a very acceptable replacement. Randle Holme, wrote his amazing text in 1649 and included endless illustrations, one of which is a drawing of a thimble that exactly resembles the thimble discussed above. Randle Holme's book was not

Plate 1. Steel scissors' cases from the collection of Henri Le Secq des Tournelles in the Museum of Rouen. The example on the left is similar to the scissors' case in Colour Plate 13. Late 17th century. From Decorative Antique Ironwork by Henry René d'Allemagne.

published until 1688 when he was described as 'Gentleman Sewer in Extraordinary to his late Majefty King Charles 2'.

Vast numbers of steel scissors and steel scissors' cases were made during the seventeenth century and an amazing collection is housed at The Museum of Rouen in France. This collection (Plate 1) was put together by Henri Le Secq des Tournelles and it spectacularly displays the tradesman's brilliant craftsmanship. Rarely are original scissors found in steel scissors' cases but these steel cases are wonderful and collectable works of art.

The late seventeenth century steel scissors' case shown in Colour Plate 13 is one of the earliest to be found fitted with a waist-clasp. It is of Flemish origin and is fitted with steel scissors from that same period. Again, as mentioned earlier, in its day it would not have been called a chatelaine. There is a marked similarity between this steel scissors' case and cases on display in The Museum of Rouen. Ironically, the steel belt hooks for scissors housed at this museum are not displayed with the scissors and scissors' cases but are in a separate showcase.

The age of oak and its accompanying heavy decoration fell into disfavour after the death of Charles II. Towards the end of the century a lighter style was introduced by artists and craftsmen brought over from Holland by William of Orange and this prepared the way for the more homely elegance of the Queen Anne period.

Colour Plate 13. Late 17th century steel scissors' case suspended by a chain from a matching waist clasp – now called a chatelaine. Contemporary steel scissors also illustrated. Flemish. c.1680. Length 8½in. (21.6cm.)

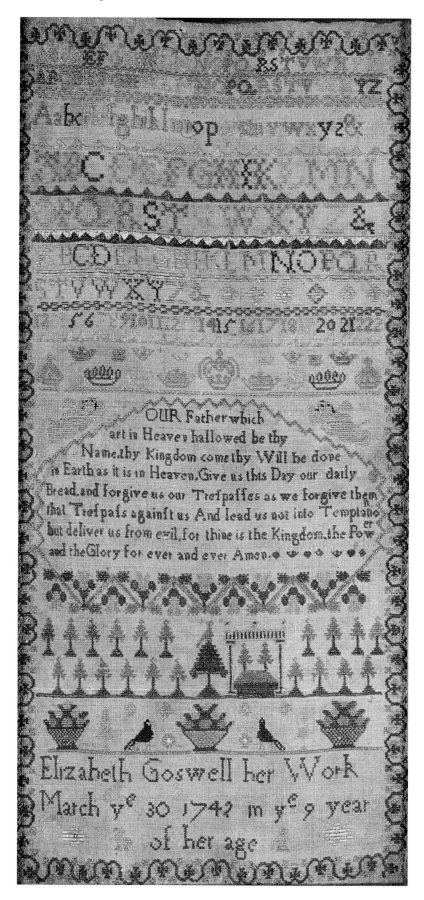

Colour Plate 16. Elizabeth Goswell's sampler worked with letters of the alphabet, numbers, crowns, birds, trees, fruit and flowers in 1742 when she was nine years old. The finely worked Lord's Prayer is flanked by angels. 18½ x 9½in. (47 x 24.2cm.)

Chapter Two

Eighteenth Century Needlework Tools & Sewing Sets

The eighteenth century brought with it a complete change in the style of furniture, furnishings and embroideries. Gone was the heavy 'stumpwork' embroidery and the heavy silver embroidery implements. Embroideries and embroidery tools became progressively lighter and daintier as the century progressed. It is rare for an embroidery, as distinct from a sampler, to be dated. However, the example illustrated (Colour Plate 14) has embroidered along the bottom 'Mary Coultman in the Year of our Lord God 1719'. The fine needlework of the central figure and animals, contrasts beautifully with the surrounding flowers worked in Algerian eye stitch. Fine embroidery, as worked by Mary Coultman, was very much the province of the upper classes. These were the ladies who owned fine embroidery tools and spent their time producing decorative items. A poor villager thought of her needle as her most treasured possession as it was needed for the necessities of life. There are, in fact, recorded instances of one needle being shared by a small village. For this level of society there was no time or place for fine decorative embroidery.

Mary Coultman, when working her fine embroidery, would no doubt have used a thimble which could have been silver and similar to the example shown in

Colour Plate 14. Embroidery by Mary Coultman dated 1719. The central figure and the animals in this embroidery have been worked in fine tent stitch contrasting with the surrounding flowers worked in Algerian eye stitch. 12 x 10in. (30.5 x 25.4cm.)

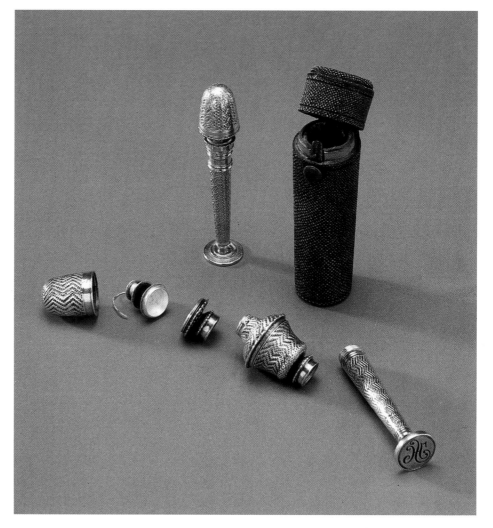

Colour Plate 17. Rear:- Silver gilt standing compendium with original shagreen case. Front:- Silver compendium showing sections - thimble, reel for thread, compartment for wax seal wafers, powder holder and needlecase with seal base. c.1720 - 1740. Height of silver gilt example 3in. (7.7cm.)

Colour Plate 15. Silver thimble found by a 'digger' at Ketsby. The thimble, initialled MH is believed to have belonged to Mary Hurd. The maker's mark can be clearly seen. c.1720.

Colour Plate 15. To locate a needlework tool with an authentic provenance is almost impossible but this silver thimble has its own fascinating story. In early 1993 a 'digger' was working on the site of a former manor house and its associated cottages at Ketsby, which is near South Ormsby in Lincolnshire near Louth. Amongst his finds was a silver thimble in amazingly good condition, initialled MH. The style of the thimble dated it to c.1720 and out of curiosity the digger decided to try to discover if anyone with those initials had lived nearby. Investigation revealed that early in the eighteenth century there had been two cottages and a farmhouse in the area being excavated. A tenant farmer was registered by the name of William Hurd. The Bishop's transcripts from the parish have a Mary Hurd born to Samuel and Elizabeth Hurd in 1713. It is not unreasonable to assume that Mary Hurd was the owner of the thimble and the grand-daughter of William Hurd. All this information has been recorded for posterity with the local museum.

Samplers, still of the narrow variety called band samplers, were worked by young girls and a knowledge of the style of sampler popular at any period of time, allows one to slot a particular sampler into a time-frame without looking at the embroidered date. The sampler in Colour Plate 16 is typical of examples worked during the 1730s and 1740s. This sampler was worked by Elizabeth Goswell in 1742 when she was nine years old and it has been framed with glass on each side.

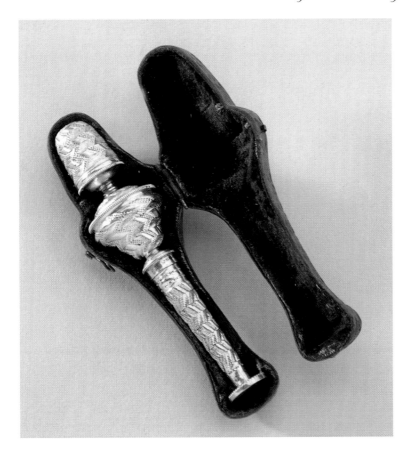

Colour Plate 18. Silver gilt standing compendium in original leather case. When unscrewed the sections are:- a thimble, reel for thread, powder holder and needlecase. c.1720 - 1740. Height of case 4½in. (11.5cm.)

This allows the back to be viewed and the embroidery is so fine and accurate the back is a perfect mirror reverse of the front. The Lord's Prayer has been embroidered in lines that increase in length and this is frequently seen in samplers embroidered with The Lord's Prayer at this time.

During the first half of the eighteenth century a standing compendium was a lady's accessory for both embroidery and writing. It is not unusual to find requirements for both of these pastimes combined, as it was considered equally important for a lady of quality to be proficient in the art of letter writing and fine embroidery. These standing compendiums, of Dutch or German origin, are made from silver or silver gilt. Occasionally they are still to be found in their original shagreen or leather cases (Colour Plates 17 & 18). The major section of these containers is a needlecase, usually with a seal base. A small compartment at the top of the needlecase is for wax wafers to be used in conjunction with the seal base. At the top of these compendiums a thimble, enclosing a small reel for thread, screws onto the wax compartment. Other variations have a vinaigrette below the thimble or a powder holder. Great care must be taken to ensure that all sections of these compendiums are matching, however, most of the decorative patterns are so distinctive a 'marriage' is very obvious. The silver gilt example in Colour Plate 18, with its original leather case, was purchased in June 1965 at a Christie's, London sale. This was the Earl of Harewood's sale of the late Princess Royal's effects. A tiny note inside one of the compartments of this compendium reads 'From Lady Mount Stephen, Xmas 1925' – presumably this was when the compendium was received as a gift.

Max von Boehn in his book *Modes and Manners – Ornaments,* features a page of designs by Johann Martin Engelbrecht dated c.1720. Included amongst these are

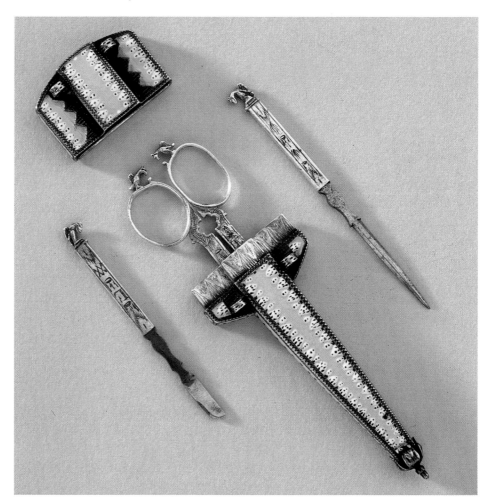

Colour Plate 19. Silver and enamel parfilage or drizzling set. The case has rings for suspension by cord from the waist. The scissors slot into the main body of the case, the knife and stiletto slot into a separate sheath in front of the scissors. Early 18th century. Length of case 3½in. (9cm.)

two ornate standing compendiums which are the earliest known designs for these implements (Plate 2).

Sets of distinctive tools are occasionally to be found in scissor-shaped cases. These tools – a pair of scissors, a stiletto and a knife – frequently have a cockerel finial. The scissors fit into the main body of the case and the other two implements fit into a sheath in front of the scissors. Rings on each side of the scissor-shaped case allow it to be worn hanging from the waist. The example (Colour Plate 19) is silver, decorated with yellow and white enamelling and thought to be of French origin.

These sets of tools were used for parfilage or drizzling as it was called in England. Parfilage was the unpicking or unravelling of silver or gold thread. Braids, tassels and embroideries from worn out coats, dresses and furnishings were stripped of their silver and gold threads before being discarded. Silver and gold recovered in this manner could be resold to tradesmen. The unravelling of gold and silver thread was considered a socially acceptable pastime by ladies of the court circle but possibly some of the stories associated with this practice are greatly exaggerated. One wonders if the ladies did besiege the gentlemen at court functions and take delight in removing gold and silver trimmings from their coats.

Plate 2. Designs by Johann Martin Engelbrecht for two ornate standing compendiums. Augsburg. c.1720. From Modes & Manners Ornaments by Max von Boehn.

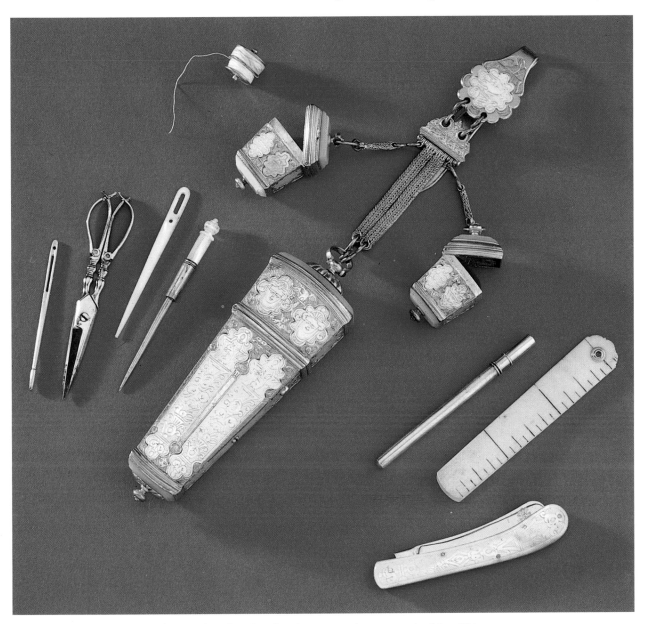

Colour Plate 20.   Gilt metal and engraved mother-of-pearl equipage – now known as a chatelaine. This chatelaine has a fully fitted central etui with implements for needlework (needlecase, scissors with folding handles, stiletto, gilt bodkin and mother-of-pearl bodkin) as well as an ivory rule and paper knife. One of the side appendages has been fitted with a pincushion while the other holds a reel for thread and has been fitted with a frame to hold a thimble. c.1730. Length 9in. (22.8cm.)

During the eighteenth century etuis were used by both men and women to hold implements thought necessary for everyday life. Many of these etuis formed the central appendage of a chatelaine (known in their day as an equipage) and some were fitted specifically with tools for embroidery. A fine example (Colour Plate 20) is of engraved mother-of-pearl and gilt metal and the etui holds a needlecase, ivory rule, penknife, scissors, stiletto, gilt and mother-of-pearl bodkins. One side appendage has a frame for a thimble and holds a double reel of silk while the other side appendage has been fitted as a pincushion. A similar fine mother-of-pearl equipage can be seen in the Jewellery Gallery of the Victoria & Albert Museum, London and is dated c.1730.

Plate 3. Trade card of H. Pugh, in Raquett-Court, Fleet-Street, London. The chatelaine in Colour Plate 21 closely resembles the example shown with only three appendages on the right of this trade card. Also illustrated are two fitted etuis. c.1740.
Courtesy: The Trustees of the British Museum.

Another gilt metal chatelaine (Colour Plate 21) was also known in its day as an equipage and it closely resembles the example on the right of H. Pugh's trade card c.1740 (Plate 3). Five similar plaited chains have been used on both examples but Mr. Pugh has chosen to illustrate only three of the appendages. The chatelaine in the colour plate has five original matching appendages that are a central case for scissors, a bodkin case, needlecase, small container fitted with a frame to hold a thimble and a matching small container that is empty. Fitted etuis can also be seen in H.Pugh's trade card and the number of eighteenth century trade cards that prominently feature these small containers confirms their popularity amongst the upper classes.

Not all etuis were made to be part of a chatelaine and many similar to the example in Colour Plate 22 have no ring attachment for suspension. This example of mother-of-pearl has a silver frame and is decorated with silver inlay. It is fitted with a thimble, folding scissors, bodkin, ear-spoon, needlecase and pencil.

Colour Plate 21. Gilt metal equipage for needlework – now known as a chatelaine – with five appendages and plaited chains. This chatelaine closely resembles an example illustrated in the Trade Card (Plate 3). The appendages are a thimble case, bodkin case, scissors' case, needlecase and an additional small container. c.1730. Length 7in. (17.8cm.)

Colour Plate 22. Mother-of-pearl bodkin case and etui. Both of these examples have been made with a silver frame and the mother-of-pearl has a delightful inlay of silver. The etui is fitted with thimble, scissors, bodkin, ear-spoon, needlecase and pencil. c.1750. Length of bodkin case 4½in. (11.5cm.)

Colour Plate 24. Rare girdle spinning wheel. The wooden 'horn' slips behind the waist band when in use as can be seen in Plate 4. c.1770. Length of horn 6¼in. (16cm.)

Colour Plate 23. Bodkin case of silver gilt filigree. There is a similarity between the designs in the filigree and needle lace from the same period of time. c.1750. Length 4¼in. (10.9cm.)

In the same colour plate the bodkin case, also mid eighteenth century, is of similar design and was of necessity large to hold bodkins of that era (Colour Plate 106). The only difference between a bodkin case and a needlecase is the size.

Another bodkin case (Colour Plate 23) has an overlay of the finest silver gilt filigree. The filigree has been made with a variety of intricate designs that look exactly like needle lace and this creates a most pleasing effect.

Stourbridge Fair, held each September in a cornfield two miles from Cambridge, was where the fashionable shopped and a likely place to purchase an extravagant trifle such as an etui. Stourbridge Fair in itself is a most interesting subject to research. Said to be the largest fair in Europe in the eighteenth century, the shops or stalls were built in rows like streets, with covered walks down which the fashionable would stroll at their leisure to inspect the goods for sale. There the glovers, silversmiths, toy sellers and lacemen set out their wares for sale. One must remember that the word 'toy' bears no similarity to the modern word for a child's plaything. 'Toy-sellers' shops sprang up at the beginning of the eighteenth century in London and were the equivalent of a modern gift shop. The word 'toy' was used to describe any small article, useful or ornamental and often of an extravagant and costly nature.

There is a drawing by Paul Sandby (c.1760) in the Royal Library at Windsor Castle of Mrs. Lane using a girdle spinning wheel (Plate 4). In this drawing Mrs. Lane can clearly be seen operating her girdle spinning wheel. In England these girdle spinning wheels were made by clock makers and when one studies the mechanism the reason for this becomes apparent.

An actual example (Colour Plate 24) appears to be of German origin and has a

Plate 4. A drawing by Paul Sandby of Mrs Lane using a girdle spinning wheel. She is drawing the flax from the distaff with her left hand while turning the handle with her right hand. The lady in the background appears to be knotting. c.1760. The Royal Library, Windsor Castle. Reproduced by gracious permission of Her Majesty the Queen.

wooden 'horn' that slips behind the waist band. From the centre of this holder and at right angles to it, a curved brass arm holds the entire spinning mechanism. This mechanism consists of two cog wheels encased in an intricately worked brass frame that is turned by a wooden handle. The flyer can be removed so that a bobbin slides onto the spindle. Unfortunately the distaff, that probably had two heads, is missing and this girdle spinning wheel would have been used for spinning or plying.

Using a girdle spinning wheel was apparently an elegant pastime for ladies and an interesting copper engraving dated 1785 of German origin shows three ladies sitting around a table spinning flax. Each of these beautifully gowned ladies are drawing flax with their left hands and turning the handles with their right hands.

During the last half of the eighteenth century England produced glorious enamelled objects – some specifically for the elegant needlewoman – and a wonderful collection can be seen at the Victoria & Albert Museum in London. Bilston (South Staffordshire) enamel thimbles in good condition are rare and the

Colour Plate 26. Enamelled etui decorated with typical naïve portraits of the 18th century. This etui was most likely made by a London maker. c.1760. Length 3¼in. (8.3cm.)

Colour Plate 27. Enamelled etui – the reverse side of Colour Plate 26, shown open to reveal the contents that include two needlework tools – a bodkin and a pair of scissors with folding handles. c.1760.

delightful example in Colour Plate 25 screws onto a combination bodkin/needlecase. Care must be taken to ensure that the sections of this accessory began life together and have not come together as a 'marriage' in recent times.

Enamelled etuis, either as an entity on their own, or as a chatelaine appendage, were fitted with needlework requisites and one such example (Colour Plates 26 & 27) is delightfully painted with naïve portraits of a lady and gentleman. This etui was most likely made by a London enameller rather than originating from the South Staffordshire area and just two of the implements it contains are for needlework – a bodkin and a pair of scissors with folding handles.

A cone-shaped enamelled etui (Colour Plates 28 & 29) holds a pair of steel scissors, bodkin and ear-spoon. These scissors are typical Georgian steel scissors and delightfully shaped. An ear-spoon was considered an essential implement to have at hand at all times and was used to remove wax from the ear. In some instances ear wax was used for waxing thread to enable thread to run more smoothly through fabric. This cone-shaped etui has been delightfully enamelled with a lady on one side and an urn of flowers on the other.

Another etui that dates from the end of the eighteenth century is in the form of a silver articulated fish (Colour Plate 30). This fish hinges open at the base of the head and the contents are revealed – scissors with folding handles, a paper knife and ear-spoon. These articulated fish were also made to hold a vinaigrette, a perfume bottle or a thimble.

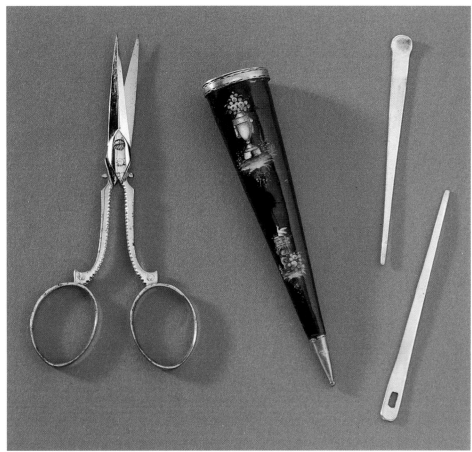

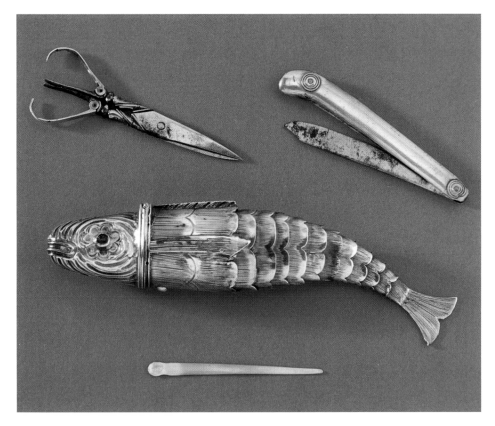

Colour Plate 28. Cone-shaped enamelled etui fitted with a frame that holds a pair of steel scissors, a bodkin and an ear-spoon. A lady with a basket of flowers has been delightfully enamelled on one side. c.1780. Length of case 3½in. (9 cm.)

Colour Plate 29. Reverse side of cone-shaped enamelled etui (Colour Plate 28) showing the contents:- typical Georgian steel scissors, ear-spoon and bodkin. This side has been enamelled with an urn of flowers and a dove. c.1780.

Colour Plate 30. Articulated silver fish that opens below the head. The contents that fit into a frame are a pair of scissors with folding handles, a paper knife and an ear-spoon. Late 18th century. Length 4¾in. (12.1cm.)

Colour Plate 34. The interior of the straw-work box shown in Colour Plate 33. The lid of this box has simple bent wire hinges and the three compartments in the top of the box have lift-up lids with similar hinges. The pictures of straw inlay have kept their vibrant colours because they have not been subjected to daylight. Late 18th century.

Chapter Three

Georgian Sewing Boxes

*I*t was not until the late eighteenth century that boxes were generally made with compartments designed specifically to hold a lady's needlework tools. Seventeenth and eighteenth century paintings often show wooden boxes, varying in size, on the floor next to a lady's chair. These unfitted boxes frequently had a padded lid that functioned as a pincushion. They were used to hold threads as well as the actual work in progress.

When visiting, embroidery and tools were often carried in beautifully embroidered draw-string bags known as pochettes (Colour Plate 31), or just the tools in their case were slipped into a pocket in the voluminous folds of the full skirts of the eighteenth century. Shallow open baskets were also used to hold skeins of silk as well as the embroidery and a small open work basket similar to the

Colour Plate 33. A magnificent straw-work box that is a fine example of prisoner-of-war work. The superb workmanship of the craftsman is apparent in every detail of this box from the urn of flowers on the lid to the detail of the oak leaves on the front of the box. It is rare to find the exterior of straw-work boxes in such good condition. Late 18th century. Width 9¼in. (23.5cm.)

Colour Plate 31. Silk pochette (draw-string bag) for carrying needlework requirements. This bag has been decorated with an edging of metallic lace and coloured sequins. Metallic thread has been couched onto the silk material to form sprays of flowers. c.1770. Length 9½in. (24.2cm.)

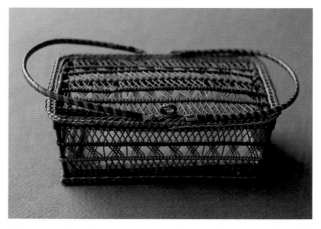

Colour Plate 32. Open-work Georgian basket of a variety used to hold small pieces of embroidery, threads and needlework tools. A silk cushion has been fitted into the base of this basket. Late 18th century. Length 10½in. (26.7cm.)

one in Colour Plate 32 could be used when visiting. A basket of this type can be seen on the table in Colour Plate 64.

During the latter part of the eighteenth century and early into the nineteenth century thousands of French prisoners of war were housed in England. Responsibility for these prisoners was violently disputed and consequently no clothes, toiletries or medical provisions were supplied, only a meagre ration of food. The prisoners were, however, allowed to make small objects to sell at a prison market and some prisoners previously skilled in various crafts were able, with the resources at hand, to fashion glorious objects. The prison at Norman Cross, near Peterborough, housed craftsmen who were specialists in straw-work and the box in Colour Plates 33 & 34 is a fine example of late eighteenth century workmanship. This box was first fashioned as a miniature wooden chest of drawers and then covered with a marquetry of fine straw-work. The lid is

Colour Plate 35. Wooden bobbin boxes were fitted with simple wire hinges and sometimes locks to protect their contents. Late 18th century. The lace bobbins are Victorian. Length of smallest box 6¾in. (17.2cm.)

Colour Plate 36. Rolled paper sewing box. An example of one of the earliest boxes made specifically for sewing. The tiny rolls of gilt-edged paper form a delightful design. This box was originally fitted with wooden barrels for thread and the two remaining barrels are shown in front of the box. Also shown is the original painted tape-measure in the shape of a house and the silk tape has been marked in nails. Late 18th century. Width 8½in. (21.6cm.)

decorated with an urn of flowers on the outside and a coastal scene on the inside. Each of the three interior compartments and the drawer are decorated with a fine marquetry straw inlay of flowers. The fineness of the workmanship of this box is not the only indicator of its age as the lid has twisted wire hinges so typical of this period of time. Although this box is not fitted for needlework it would have been used by a lady to hold a combination of toiletries and sewing tools. Straw-work continued to be a popular craft well into the nineteenth century and not all available pieces can be designated as prisoner of war work.

Simple twisted wire hinges were also used on small wooden boxes that held lace bobbins and these wire hinges can be seen on the smaller bobbin box in Colour Plate 35. These plain bobbin boxes date from the end of the eighteenth century and into the early part of the nineteenth century. Written on the inside of the lid of the box at the rear of this same colour plate is the instruction 'This is for Sarah Ann Boon when I die. Mary Boon'. A small collection of wooden bobbins are also shown in this colour plate and although these bobbins appear to be a later date than the bobbin box, one of the bobbins is inscribed 'Eli Boon'.

The end of the twentieth century has seen the revival of a craft now known as quilling. This craft uses rolled slivers of paper to make a picture on a firm background. There is no doubt the idea for this craft had its beginnings late in the eighteenth century when rolled paper work was a meticulous craft. Jane Austen's novel *Sense and Sensibility* was written in November, 1797 and the author must have been very aware of this pastime when she has her character Elinor Dashwood offering to help Lucy Steel by rolling papers for the basket she is making. The sewing box in Colour Plate 36 is a superb example of the fine workmanship required to produce a top quality rolled paper box. This wooden framed box has been decorated with tiny rolls of gilt-edged paper firmly packed together. The shaping of the rolls of paper form a delightful pattern. This box has

Colour Plate 37. Pen-and-ink work sewing box. The lid of this box has a wide decorative border of this craft. This box has been fitted specifically for sewing and the remaining original tools are displayed in front of the box. They are three wooden cotton barrels, four wooden reels for thread and a very rare early wooden thimble with a painted band. c.1800. Width 9in. (22.8cm.)

been fitted as a sewing box and inside at the front has a roller with a ratchet – a requirement for netting. The heavy lead weighted base of this box would allow the foundation loop required for netting to be attached to the roller and kept taut. The fittings in this box are made of wood and include a multiple reel, two barrels to hold thread and a painted wooden tape-measure in the form of a round house with a silk tape marked in 'nails'. The English yard has been a standard measurement of length ever since King Henry I decided it should be the length of his arm. This yard length and its fractions are sometimes marked on early silk tapes. Thus a ribbon may be marked Q for Quarter, H for Half Yard and Y for Yard. To indicate a smaller measure than a quarter yard a measure of two and a quarter inches was marked and called a Nail. Thus a tape may be marked 1 Nail, 2 Nails etc.

English sewing boxes decorated with pen-and-ink work were popular c.1800

Colour Plate 38. Stained horn and decorated ivory sewing box with a sandalwood interior. These boxes were made in Vizagapatam in East India for the increasing European population. Late 18th century. Width 10in. (25.4cm.)

and the box in Colour Plate 37 is a typical example. The lid of this box has a wide decorative border of pen-and-ink work and a narrow band of this craft borders the central medallion. This medallion depicts a mother sitting at a spinet with a small child on her lap. The tray inside this box has been fitted with a roller on a ratchet for netting and the needlework tools displayed in front of the box are typical for this era. These tools are three wooden barrels as well as reels for thread – the reels have painted navy bands to match the coloured bands on the very rare early painted Tunbridge wooden thimble.

Another late eighteenth century sewing box originated from Vizagapatam in East India. This box (Colour Plate 38) is of stained horn and ivory and the interior of sandalwood still retains its characteristic aroma. A tray in this box lifts out and its compartments have distinctive ivory lids decorated with a black floral pattern. Vizagapatam was the site of an East India Company factory and products based on European designs were produced there from 1756 to cater for the increasing

Colour Plate 39. Ivory sewing box with a fine flower and leaf decoration of black lac. The claw feet are typical for this period of time. c.1800. Width 7¾in. (19.8cm.)

European population of an area stretching from the Bay of Bengal to the Coromandel Coast. Vast quantities of superb articles were purchased there by Lord Clive and the Clive Collection can be viewed at Powis Castle near Welshpool in Wales. A letter, written by Henrietta Clive to her father on 4th April, 1801 while visiting Vizagapatam with her mother and sister, solves a lot of questions regarding the black decoration on the ivory of these boxes. Henrietta writes:-

'We have seen the people inlaying the ivory it appears very simple they draw the pattern… they intend with a pencil and then cut it out slightly with a small piece of Iron, they afterwards put hot Lac upon it, and when it is dry scrape it off and polish it, the Lac remains in the marks made with the piece of Iron…'

To understand Henrietta's letter more fully the dictionary meaning of the word Lac is:-

A resinous substance secreted by a scale insect (Tachardia Lacca) widely cultivated, especially in Northern India. This resin is melted, purified, and then solidified in thin layers, which form the shellac of commerce.

Ivory decorated with Lac in this manner can be seen on another Indian box (Colour Plates 39 & 40). The ivory on this box has been veneered onto a wooden

Colour Plate 40. Interior of ivory sewing box shown in Colour Plate 39, showing the sandalwood lining and exquisite ivory fretwork motif under the lid. There are compartments for cotton barrels on either side of the two ivory thimbles at the back of the box. Two sections are fitted with red velvet pincushions and the front of the box has a multiple reel. The three remaining compartments have decorated ivory lids. c.1800.

carcass and the box lined with sandalwood. The interior fittings – a multiple reel and thimbles – are of ivory. The empty compartments on either side of the thimbles would have originally held ivory cotton barrels. Red velvet has been used for pincushions. A delightful final touch is the fretted ivory vignette on the inside of the lid. This box has the typical ivory claw feet of c.1800.

Leather clad sewing boxes that are distinctively English were also made c.1800. Brass feet, rings and lions' heads on each end and a brass plaque on the lid contrast beautifully with the red or black leather. These boxes were made in a variety of sizes and the box in Colour Plate 41 has a compartmented lift out tray with room underneath for small pieces of embroidery. This tray has spaces to fit specific needlework tools. The smaller red leather boxes in Colour Plate 42 have

Colour Plate 41. Red leather Georgian sewing box. Brass feet, rings and lion's head are typical fittings for these leather boxes that were also covered in green or black leather. The ivory cotton barrels shown in front of the box are typical fittings. c.1800. Width 10¼in. (26.1cm.)

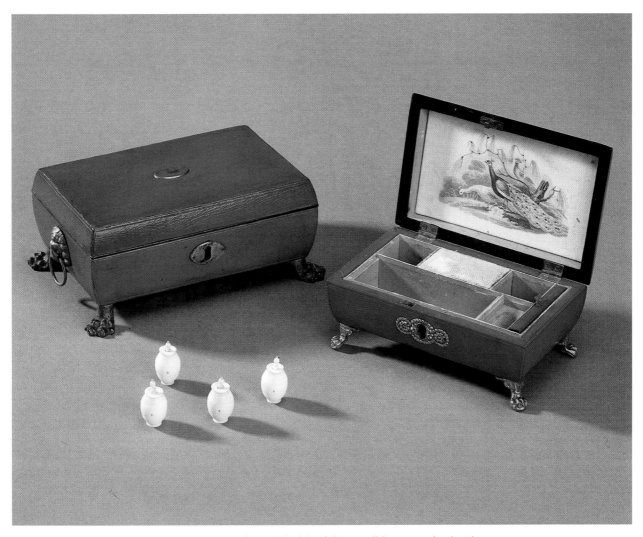

Colour Plate 42. Two red leather Georgian sewing boxes. The lids of these small boxes were lined with silk that was often engraved with a picture, in this case that of a group of peacocks. One compartment of the smaller box has been fitted with a pincushion, there is a recess to hold a thimble and a red leather needlebook slots into a cavity on the right hand side of the box. Ivory cotton barrels were typical fittings. c.1800. Width 5¾in. (14.6cm.)

engravings on silk inside their lids and one of these boxes is fitted with matching ivory cotton barrels, steel scissors, needlecase and stiletto.

As a general rule Georgian sewing boxes were fitted with ivory tools, boxes from the Victorian era with mother-of-pearl tools and the Edwardian period is synonymous with sterling silver tools. Of course there are exceptions to this general rule – for example, while ivory fitted sewing boxes were popular during the Georgian era in England, mother-of-pearl fitted boxes from the Palais Royal were the height of fashion in France.

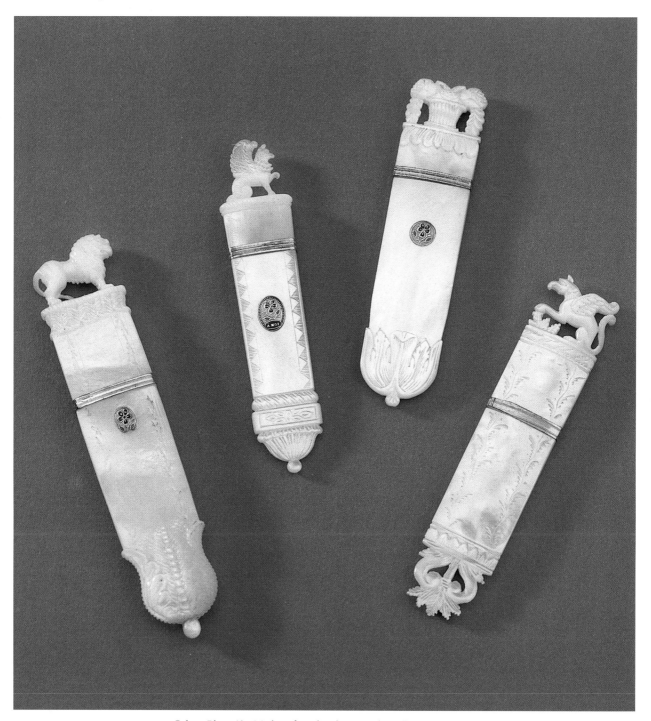

Colour Plate 43. Mother-of-pearl Palais Royal needlecases. These glorious examples show the variety of decorative finials as well as the fine engraving on the body of the needlecases. Three of these needlecases have the enamelled pansy plaque that was the symbol of the Palais Royal. c.1800. Length of longest 4in. (10.2cm.)

Chapter Four

The Palais Royal

The most prestigious sewing box sought by collectors of needlework tools is the box known as the Palais Royal Sewing Box. To understand the 'aura' attached to these boxes, it is necessary to understand some of the history attached to the Palais Royal.

This Palace was built in Paris in 1629 for Cardinal Richelieu and at that time was called the Palais Cardinal. During the eighteenth century, Louis Philippe d'Orléans inherited this palace and, as a clever business venture, rebuilt one wing, turning it into an arcade of shops and restaurants bordering a magnificent garden. Renaming the building the Palais Royal, the shops were occupied in the late 1780s. Only the best quality articles were sold at the Palais Royal – artisans displayed their wares in ideal surroundings, and it became the place 'to be seen'. To promenade there was an evening's ultimate entertainment.

Palais Royal sewing boxes are filled with the most wonderful delicate mother-of-pearl tools, and the most prestigious are set with an enamel pansy or *pensée*, meaning thought, or 'think of me'. Although the Palais Royal and mother-of-pearl tools are synonymous, occasionally ivory needlework tools are found fitted with an enamel pansy.

Colour Plate 44. Mother-of-pearl silk winders from Palais Royal boxes. These winders were made in an enormous variety of designs and are truly works of art. It is obvious why the smallest are called snowflakes. One winder still holds a small quantity of silver thread. c.1800. Diameter of largest 1¾in. (4.5cm.)

A great variety of boxes were sold at the Palais Royal. The most usual are made of satinwood in a variety of sizes, and quite often the exterior of the box would be decorated with steel. Some of these boxes were made in the shape of a miniature spinet, and frequently a music box was part of the fittings.

The implements were made by specialists in their fields, and this accounts for the fact that there is no uniform pattern in Palais Royal boxes. A scissors specialist would have his scissors fashioned with flowered mother-of-pearl handles, which would complement the shell pattern used by the maker of needlecases. A specialist box maker would gather together his selection of tools, and a box would be made to ensure that each tool fitted firmly into its own recessed compartment. It is very hard to find Palais Royal boxes with all their compartments fitted with the original pieces. It is inevitable that at some time during the last two centuries, an owner would have used one particular tool and not replaced it in the box.

Some boxes still carry the maker's label with the prestigious Palais Royal address – but a Palais Royal box does not need a maker's label to identify it – the superb workmanship leaves no one in doubt as to its origin.

These boxes did not only hold sewing tools. It was the custom at the end of the eighteenth century for other tools to be incorporated into a Palais box.

Firstly, examining the tools not associated with needlework, the ear-spoon is the most commonly found implement. As strange as it may seem to us today, during the eighteenth and early nineteenthth century people found it absolutely imperative to have a tiny spoon always at hand to clean wax from their ears. Quite often, tweezers are at the other end of this tiny implement. More to our liking are the lovely cut-glass perfume bottles with gold or silver-gilt tops which slot into the recess made exactly to fit their shape.

Writing implements also played an important part in the fittings of a Palais box. Sometimes a steel curved blade fitted with a mother-of-pearl handle is found and this knife was used for lifting seals. A round, flat mother-of-pearl box that held wax seal wafers and a seal may be found and this may carry either initials or a family crest.

A vast range of needlework tools can be found in various boxes – a mother-of-pearl thimble with an enamelled pansy is the tool most prized by collectors. These thimbles, with one or two bands of gold or silver-gilt are rarely in perfect condition, as cracks develop along the striations of the mother-of-pearl. Scissors with steel blades and mother-of-pearl handles come in a variety of designs. The handles may be adorned with flowers or mermaids – but the ultimate are the scissors where the handles are carved mother-of-pearl serpents with their tails in their mouths, this motif being the symbol of eternity. Some of these scissors have the enamel pansy motif. A needlecase of mother-of-pearl will fit into its exact place. These needlecases have beautifully carved finials – some a basket of flowers, or a swan – here again the variety is endless. The ultimate test as to whether the piece is original is if it fits the recess exactly and 'has the right feel'. A stiletto was a must, as so much embroidery necessitated the use of this implement, and a Palais

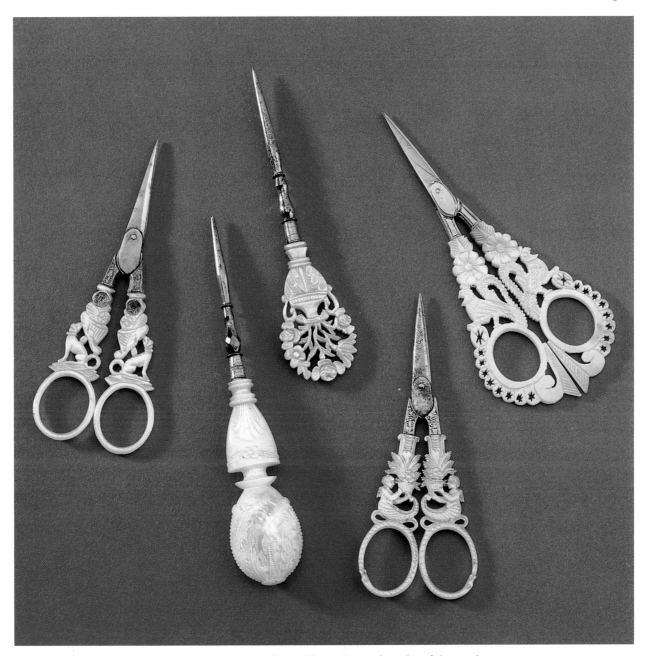

Colour Plate 45. Scissors and stilettos from Palais Royal boxes. The intricate workmanship of the carved mother-of-pearl is especially apparent in the handles of the scissors. One pair has the enamelled pansy plaques, the symbol of the Palais Royal. c.1800. Length of longest stiletto 4¾in. (12.1cm.)

box always held a bodkin. This bodkin may be of gold, silver-gilt or gloriously carved mother-of-pearl.

Silk winders – flat mother-of-pearl discs – are probably the most exquisite implements to be found. These winders, with their intricate carved decoration, may be only half an inch (1.3 cm.) in diameter and are called snowflakes for obvious reasons. They sit on a rim of chenille in a recess that has a mirror base. A pair of tiny reels for holding thread are sometimes included as fittings. Another tool that is occasionally found in Palais boxes is a mother-of-pearl tambour hook, tambouring being the height of elegance at this period. Collecting these individual mother-of-pearl tools is delightful, as can be seen in Colour Plates 43, 44, & 45.

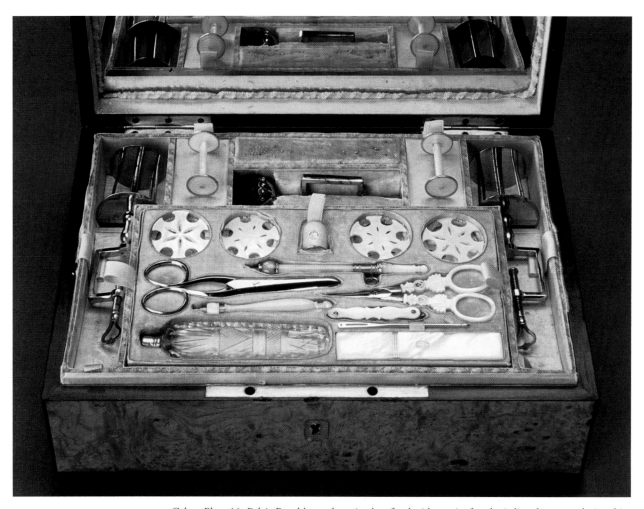

Colour Plate 46. Palais Royal burr ash sewing box fitted with a pair of steel winding clamps, steel pincushion clamp and steel scissors – all in excellent condition. The other fittings, of mother-of-pearl, are a pair of reels, four winders, a thimble, tambour hook, scissors, crochet hook and needlecase. A bodkin, perfume bottle and ear-spoon/toothpick complete the fittings in the box. The hollow section under the tray is fitted with a music box. The box bears the label 'Hebert of Paris'. c.1810. Length 11in. (28cm.)

Some rare Palais boxes (Colour Plate 46) are fitted with steel clamps as well as a selection of mother-of-pearl tools. Compartments have been made at each end of the tray in this box to hold a pair of steel winding clamps. A third steel clamp, with a pincushion top, fits into its compartment at the back of the box in front of a fitted pincushion. These steel clamps, as well as the steel scissors, are in excellent condition – something quite rare for steel tools of this age. A mother-of-pearl reel fits into a recess on each side of the pincushion clamp and for this photograph they have been placed on top of the lids that would normally give them a protective covering. This box also has four mother-of-pearl winders for silk thread, a mother-of-pearl thimble with its prestigious enamel pansy, a mother-of-pearl crochet hook, as well as a mother-of-pearl tambour hook. The mother-of-pearl handled pair of scissors and the mother-of-pearl needlecase are also fitted with an enamel pansy. A bodkin, perfume bottle and combination ear-spoon/tooth pick complete the fittings in this box. The hollow section of the box under the lift-out tray is fitted with a music box that is original and in excellent condition. Additionally, this box still bears the label of the prestigious firm of Hebert, Paris.

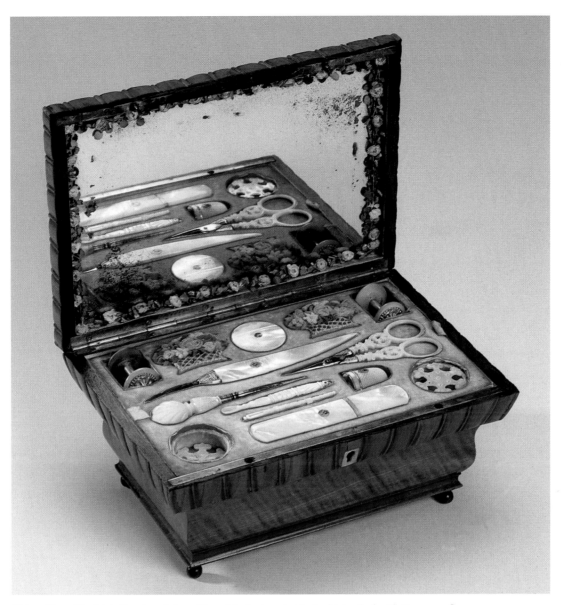

Colour Plate 47. Palais Royal work box. The original mirror inside the lid is edged with tiny paper flowers that complement the two embroidered pincushion baskets of flowers at the back of the tray of the box. The tools for needlework are a pair of mother-of-pearl and gilt reels, scissors, stiletto, bodkin, thimble, needlecase and two winders. Other implements are an ear-spoon with toothpick, a seal knife and round box for holding wax seal wafers. The music box fitted into the base plays two tunes. c.1800. Width 8¼in. (22.4cm.)

Palais boxes usually have a mirror inside the lid and this mirror is almost always edged with chenille. However, occasionally tiny paper flowers were used as an edging as can be seen in Colour Plate 47. The owner or owners of this box obviously thought the pincushions were too delightful to use. They are exquisitely embroidered baskets of flowers still in pristine condition whereas the box does show evidence of use. This particular box has an array of tools for needlework – two reels, scissors, stiletto, thimble, bodkin, two winders and a needlecase. It also has an ear-spoon that incorporates a silver tooth pick and two implements for writing – a seal knife and a round box for holding seal wafers. A music box is fitted into the base of the box under the lift-out tray and this particular music box plays two tunes.

Colour Plate 48. A superb Palais Royal box of simulated coromandel in a casket shape with a lid inlaid with mother-of-pearl flowers. One of the finest examples of Palais Royal boxes. c.1810. Width 8¾in. (22.4cm.)

Colour Plate 49. Interior of Palais Royal box shown in Colour Plate 48. The mirror inside the lid has been edged with tiny paper flowers and wax flowers have been used to decorate the pincushion at the back of the tray of the box. The needlework tools in this box are a set of four winders, a bodkin, thimble, scissors, stiletto and needlecase. The other implements are a seal, round seal wafer box, ear-spoon and a glass perfume bottle. The box has a silk lined section under the tray to hold small pieces of embroidery. c.1810.

The Palais box in Colour Plates 48 & 49 is in superb condition. The exterior is quite rare as it is of simulated coromandel with a fine inlay of mother-of-pearl flowers in the centre of the domed lid. This box also has tiny paper flowers around the mirror in perfect condition – an amazing fact when one considers the age of the box (c.1800).

The pincushion in this box has been decorated with wax flowers and, like the rest of the box, is in excellent condition. The mother-of-pearl sewing tools in this box are a set of four matching winders, bodkin, thimble, scissors, stiletto and needlecase. Other implements are a seal, round seal wafer box, ear-spoon and a glass perfume bottle. The tools are fitted into a lift-out tray so that small pieces of fine embroidery could be kept in the silk lined base.

Colour Plate 50. The pièce de résistance *of the Palais Royal box shown in Colour Plates 48 and 49. This original embroidered cushion, edged with chenille, fits over the tray of implements to give protection. c.1810. Width 7½in. (19.1cm.)*

The *pièce de résistance* of this particular Palais Royal box is the wonderful embroidered cushion that fits over the needlework tools as a protection. (Colour Plate 50) These cushions are found in most Palais boxes and are usually edged with matching chenille to that used in the box. They are quite often exquisite examples of ribbon embroidery and are a work of art in their own right.

Another Palais Royal box (Colour Plate 51) is a tremendous contrast to the previous two boxes discussed as it is very restrained in style although its plain lines give it a quiet elegance. The tray of this box has been lined with grey velvet and silk – the pincushions are a darker grey velvet. The silk cushion, not shown, is also made from matching grey silk and edged with white chenille that matches the chenille surrounding the mirror inside the lid. Four matching mother-of-pearl winders for silk thread slot into recesses that have mirror bases edged with the same white chenille. A folding mother-of-pearl rule at the back of the box allows

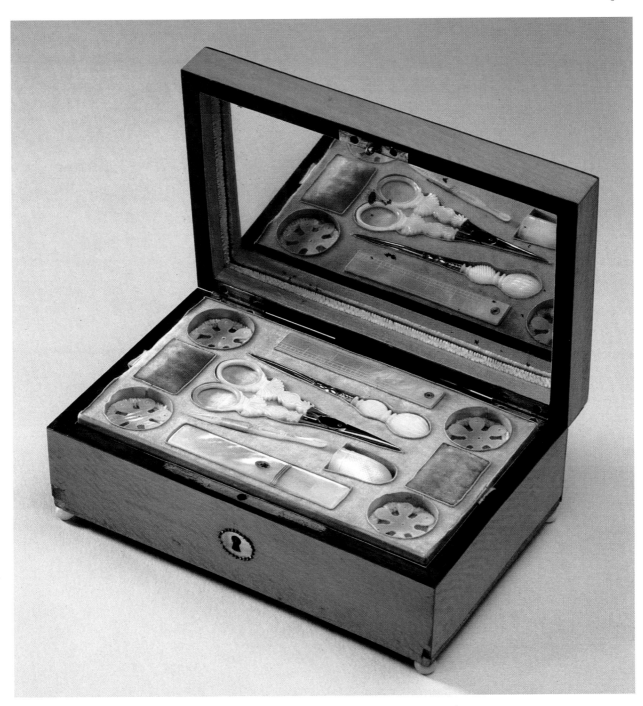

Colour Plate 51. Satinwood Palais Royal sewing box in a more restrained elegant style. Two practical grey pincushions are fitted on either side of the mother-of-pearl tools that are a folding rule, stiletto, scissors, bodkin/ear-spoon, thimble, needlecase and four winders. c.1810. Width 7¾in. (19.8cm.)

a lady to measure her work in progress up to eleven inches (28 cm.). The other needlework tools are a mother-of-pearl handled stiletto, a pair of mother-of-pearl handled scissors, mother-of-pearl bodkin/ear-spoon, mother-of-pearl thimble and mother-of-pearl needlecase that has an enamel pansy motif. The lid of this satinwood box is beautifully decorated with cut steel matching the escutcheon around the key-hole. This box was originally fitted with a music box which is sadly now missing.

Colour Plate 52. *Gilt metal and engraved mother-of-pearl Palais Royal box with scrolling gilt handles and gilt cupids decorating each side. The lid has been fitted with a painting under glass. c.1810. Width 5¾in. (14.6cm.)*

Colour Plate 53. *Interior of Palais Royal box shown in Colour Plate 52. The tray of this box has a painted pincushion at the back and fittings of either mother-of-pearl or gold that look exactly 'right' for this box. Two winders, two reels and a thimble are of mother-of-pearl while the needlecase, bodkin, scissors and stiletto are of gold. A glass perfume bottle with a gold lid completes the fittings. The thimble has an enamelled pansy. c.1810.*

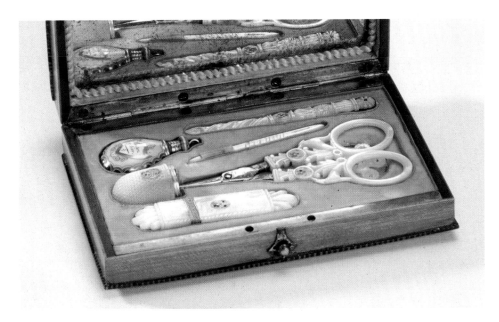

Not all Palais Royal boxes are large in size – many were small rectangular wooden boxes, the lids often decorated with cut steel. Very occasionally one finds a Palais box with a gilt metal frame and sides of engraved mother-of-pearl. The box in Colour Plates 52 & 53 is a glorious example of this variety and for added attraction the lid has been fitted with a painting under glass. The fittings are either gold (needlecase, bodkin, scissors and stiletto) or have a gold trim (silk winders, thimble, reels and the cap of the perfume bottle). The mother-of-pearl thimble is the only implement decorated with an enamel pansy. The pincushion at the rear of the box has been decorated with a painting of flowers. The tray holding the needlework tools lifts out and the empty section underneath can be used to hold threads or small pieces of embroidery. The mirror inside the lid is original and has been edged with chenille.

A small work box of burr amboyna was made in the form of a book (Colour Plates 54 & 55). A clever line inlay and chequered border creates this 'book' appearance and the 'spine' divides when the book is opened along a matching inlaid band. The lid is fitted with an internal mirror and a silk pad protects the fittings. The scissors, needlecase, thimble and ear-spoon are inset with an enamel pansy – the symbol of the Palais Royal, and additional needlework tools are a mother-of-pearl silk winder and bodkin. An exquisite pink porcelain pear-shaped scent bottle, inscribed 'Penser y Bien', completes the contents. So called 'secret books' were popular tokens of love amongst the court circle of Charles X.

For sheer beauty the Palais Royal box in its entirety surpasses all other sewing boxes and it is understandable why it is considered the ultimate sewing box.

Colour Plate 54. A small box of burr amboyna made in the form of a book. A clever inlay creates the book appearance and the spine divides when the box is opened. A small mother-of-pearl plaque has been fitted into the front of the box. c.1820. Width 5in. (12.7cm.)

Colour Plate 56. Colifichet embroidery of parrots in a fruit tree. These double-sided embroideries are worked in satin stitch in shades of silk on a heavy paper that is like parchment. English. c.1770.

Chapter Five

Georgian Crafts

The most beautiful and elegant fine embroidery dates from the Georgian era. In fact, this is the era when ladies produced a wide range of exquisite crafts. It is also the age of Mrs Mary Delany (1700-1788) who has to be considered the 'matriarch' of all hand crafts. Her whole life was devoted to producing wonderful creations and she is probably best known for her paper cuts of flowers or 'paper mosaics' but embroidery and knotting were among her passions.

Some wonderful embroideries have been preserved from this time. Possibly the ones that delight and mystify collectors the most are double-sided embroideries, worked in shades of silk on paper and known as Colifichets. Unless great care was taken when this embroidery was undertaken the heavy paper, like parchment, would split along the track made by the needle. However, some glorious examples of this technique have survived and Colour Plates 56 & 57 show both sides of one particular embroidery. The side of this superb embroidery that has been subjected to light is faded while the other side retains its vibrant colours. Worked in a smooth double-sided satin stitch the skill required to achieve identical work on each side of the paper is superlative. Louis de Farcy, writing just before 1914, stated that Colifichets were worked by nuns in the Visitation

Colour Plate 57. The reverse side of the colifichet embroidery (Colour Plate 56) that has obviously been subjected to sunlight. The exacting nature of this embroidery can be clearly seen by examining these two colour plates. Great care is needed to stop the paper splitting along the track made by the needle. English. c.1770. Embroidery 9½ x 8½in. (24.2 x 21.6cm.)

Colour Plate 58. Silk embroidery of a lass with her fishing basket, rod, line and fish. These popular embroideries were sold with the picture already drawn on the background silk and the hands, faces and sky delicately painted. English. Late 18th century. Width, including frame, 8in. (20.3cm.)

Convent at Loudon in France in the eighteenth century. St. Aubin also states 'Some Religious Communities embroider shaded baskets and bouquets of flowers in flat silk on both sides of heavy paper (collé fiché).' Margaret Swain in her research discovered that 'the two elder daughters of the 4th Earl of Traquair had been sent to Paris in 1713 to finish their education. On May 16, 1714 Lady Anne Stuart wrote to her mother :- '...as for works, wee have learned the coly fishes, and to make purses...' Further research by M. Swain identified the convent that Lady Anne attended as the Ursuline Convent of St. Jacques, Paris, a convent known for its embroidery. Perhaps the precision of embroidering colifichets was considered excellent preparation for the fine workmanship of religious embroideries, but this delicate embroidery was not only produced in Convents. This form of embroidery was also popular in England and the example being discussed is thought to be of English origin from the third quarter of the eighteenth century. Although not embroidered, Mrs Delany produced paper cuts of similar exotic birds at this same period of time and these are featured on page 100 of the delightful book – *Mrs Delany her life and her flowers* by Ruth Hayden.

Embroidery, like all crafts, goes through cycles of popularity. The end of the twentieth century has seen a revival of painting on fabric being combined with embroidery. What is interesting is that this combination was popular at the end of the nineteenth century and in particular at the end of the eighteenth century.

Colour Plate 59. Sentimental silk embroidery of 'Fame adorning Shakespeare's Tomb' taken from the painting by the Swiss artist Angelica Kauffman and worked mainly in long and satin stitch. Late 18th century. Width, including frame, 10½in. (26.7cm.)

These late eighteenth century silk embroideries were very much a leisure pursuit of the upper classes. They are pictorial embroideries worked mainly with silk and chenille threads on a silk background. A distinctive feature of these 'pictures' is the painted sky and the figures usually have delicately painted faces, hands and arms. As one studies and views more and more of these silk embroideries, it becomes apparent that there is a repetitiveness in the subjects and scenes. In fact, certain scenes are seen so frequently that one comes to the correct conclusion that they were mass-produced. Indeed, such was the case, as they were sold in kits, frequently with the sky and faces, hands and arms of the figures already painted.

Because of the repetitiveness of the scenes of surviving silk embroideries we are well able to judge what was so very popular at this time. Pastoral scenes abounded, albeit idyllic, reproducing an imagined ideal world. A shepherdess with her sheep is one such example and the inspiration for this embroidery was taken from a Bartolozzi engraving. A maid sitting spinning is a popular theme while a rarer one is the young lady shown with a fishing line having just caught a fish (Colour Plate 58).

Sentimentality was at its height and the painting 'Fame adorning Shakespeare's Tomb' by the Swiss artist Angelica Kauffman (1741–1807) shows a classically draped female strewing flowers on a tomb. This is a mourning picture that must have been extremely popular and although usually worked in coloured embroidery (Colour Plate 59), the example in Colour Plate 60 is so finely

Colour Plate 60. Black silk embroidery of 'Fame' in a similar pose to Colour Plate 59. This embroidery is worked so finely in a stipple effect that at first glance it appears to be a print. The stipple effect has been achieved by the random placing of tiny black stitches. Late 18th century. Width 5in. (12.7cm.)

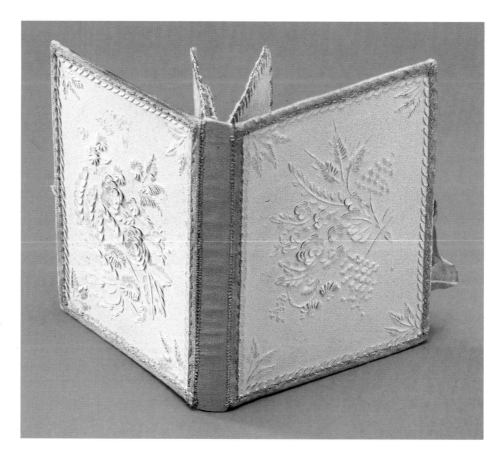

Colour Plate 62. Needlebook of cream board edged with blue silk. The cream board covers of this needlebook have been cut to produce raised leaves and flowers. Flannel pages edged with blue blanket stitch hold a selection of needles. c.1800. Height 3in. (7.7cm.)

Colour Plate 61. Rare hair embroidery of Rembrandt. The embroiderer has created a brilliant representation of the artist worked entirely with strands of hair mainly in random cross stitch. Embroideries are usually only partly worked with hair. Late 18th century. Size of embroidery 5 x 3½in. (12.7 x 9cm.)

worked with black silk in a stipple effect, that at first glance it appears to be a print.

Not to be confused with these print-like embroideries are the rarer examples worked with hair. Usually when hair is used in an embroidery the greater part of the picture is worked in silk thread. It is extremely rare to find an embroidery worked entirely with hair of different shades. One such example (Colour Plate 61) depicts the bust of Rembrandt and is of the finest workmanship dating from the last quarter of the eighteenth century. It is not difficult to differentiate between hair and silk threads. A strand of hair, seen through a strong magnifying glass, exactly resembles nylon fishing line as distinct from the textured outline of silk threads.

It is against this wonderful craft background of the Georgian era, that ladies so talented with a needle and thread, produced exquisite hand-made needlebooks and pincushions. One such needlebook (Colour Plate 62) is reminiscent of the work of Mrs Delany, as the cream board on each side of the needlebook has been cut to produce a floral pattern – the tiny, cut petals raised to achieve a delightful three-dimensional effect. Tiny stitches have been used to edge each cover with blue silk and bind them into a book.

Scraps of silk material left over from the beautiful gowns of the late eighteenth century were never wasted. Frequently they were used to make pincushions and

Colour Plate 63. Hand made silk pincushions. The largest, decorated with tufts of metallic thread at each corner, is possibly made from Spitalfield silk and is late 18th century. The small boot and shoe silk pincushions have minute stitching and date from the late 18th/early 19th century. Length of shoe 2¼in. (5.8cm.)

one such example, possibly of Spitalfield silk, has tufts of metallic thread at each corner. Silk shoe and boot-shaped pincushions were exquisitely made with the tiniest stitches. These early pincushions (Colour Plate 63) often still retain their original pins which are quite distinctive, as the head and the shaft of the pin was made from two separate pieces of wire – something that can clearly be seen through a magnifying glass – in fact, in some cases with the naked eye.

The gentle art of knotting was a popular pastime amongst ladies of the upper classes and the court circle during the last half of the eighteenth century. Paintings from this period often show ladies with their shuttles poised to begin the next knot – the completed knotted thread disappearing into a beautifully embroidered bag (similar to the pochette in Colour Plate 31) hanging from their left wrists. Unlike a tatting shuttle, a knotting shuttle does not have tight points, in fact there is a large opening at each end of the shuttle. This is so that coarse fibre as well as fine silk thread can be wound around the central post because it is the diameter of the thread that determines the size of the knot and not the size of the shuttle. Knotting is achieved by holding the shuttle in the right hand and passing it through a loop of thread held in the left hand thus producing a series of knots along the thread similar to a string of pearls. The knots can be placed close together or quite a distance apart. Sir Joshua Reynolds' painting of 'Anne, Countess of Albemarle' (Colour Plate 64) was completed by 1760. In this portrait Anne is seen knotting – a typical pose for that era. The knotted thread can be clearly seen as can the space between the points at the end of her shuttle. Of particular interest is the open-work basket at her elbow that is holding a ball of thread.

Mrs Delany was one of the greatest exponents of knotting and frequently referred to current projects in her letters. Writing to her sister in 1750 she says '.... I am knotting to trim a new blue and white linen bed I have just put up ....' One of the ways Mrs Delany used knotting was as an outline for flowers and leaves, couching the knotted thread down onto a background material.

Knotting shuttles are probably the most glorious *objets d'art* of all needlework implements. Although some shuttles were made of tortoiseshell or ivory without

Colour Plate 64. Portrait of Anne, Countess of Albemarle, by Sir Joshua Reynolds completed by 1760. The Countess is shown knotting and the space between the points at the end of her shuttle can be clearly seen. The openwork basket on the table is of particular interest.

Reproduced by courtesy of the Trustees, The National Gallery, London.

Colour Plate 65. Gold knotting shuttle with enamelled pastoral scenes made in Paris by J.J. Barrière in 1769-70. This is a superb knotting shuttle and any collector visiting London should view it and the other examples shown in Plates 5, 6 & 7 housed at The Wallace Collection in London. Length 4½in. (11.5cm.)

adornment, the majority were expensive and exquisite works of art. Mrs. Delany frequently wrote about her friendship with King George III and Queen Charlotte and in 1783 records 'The King ...presented me with a gold knotting shuttle, of the most exquisite workmanship and taste...' Some of the most magnificent knotting shuttles are displayed in The Wallace Collection in London. Here one can view a three colour gold shuttle decorated with flowers made by J.V.Huguet in 1757-8. Another, from the same era, is of cut steel partly gilt, another is of rock crystal but the *pièce de résistance* is a gold shuttle with enamelled pastoral scenes made in Paris by J.J. Barrière in 1769 - 70 (Plates 5, 6 & 7, and Colour Plate 65). There have always been two trains of thought as to why knotting was so popular as a social pastime amongst ladies of the upper class. Firstly, it was a most flattering occupation as it required little concentration and full attention could be given to one's pose and exaggerated affectations. However, the other train of thought gives credence to the idea that it was considered ungodly to have idle hands. Madame de Genlis (Stéphanie-Felicité Ducrest de Saint-Aubin) was born in Burgundy in 1746 and became lady-in-waiting to the Duchesse d'Orléans in 1769. Later in her life, after the French Revolution, she wrote a dictionary of etiquette from her personal recollections of the French court. Under 'navettes' (the French word for knotting shuttle) she writes – 'formerly women, to have a good appearance while making.visits, or in an intimate group, drew from their work-bags a pretty navette of gold, shell or ivory and began to knot. This work in general was of no practical use, but was a sort of emblem expressing the aversion of all women to total idleness.' It is interesting that Madame de Genlis remarks '...the work in general was of no practical use...' as it appears the French, in contrast to the English, made little use of their completed knotting.

Numerous tradesmen in London advertised shuttles for knotting during the last half of the eighteenthth century. The trade card for Riccard and Littlefear's Manufactory (collection Guildhall Library, London) advertises 'Shuttles for Knotting, etc, made in Mother-o' Pearl, Tortoiefhell, Steel and Ivory' and a bill of sale that has been hand written on the back of this trade card has been dated 1783.

Plate 5. Three colour gold knotting shuttle decorated with flowers. Made in Paris by J. V. Huguet in 1757-8. Length 4¾in. (12.1 cm.)

Plate 6. Steel knotting shuttle partly gilt with a monogram of V and interlaced Ls. Possibly owned by Madame Victoire (1733-99) daughter of Louis XV. French. c. 1750-75. Length 5¾in. (14.6cm.)

Plate 7. Rock crystal knotting shuttle with gold and garnet screw heads. Made in Paris in 1768-9. Length 5in. (12.7cm.)

These three shuttles reproduced by permission of the Trustees of the Wallace Collection.

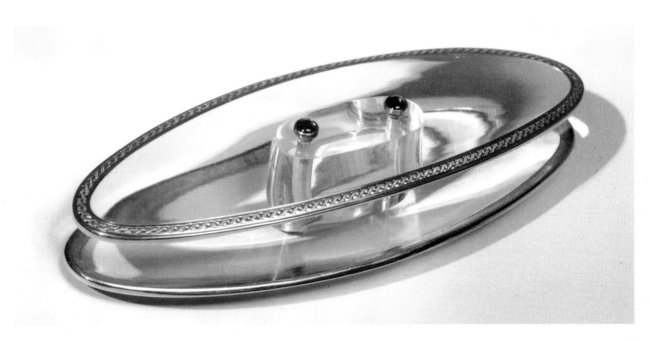

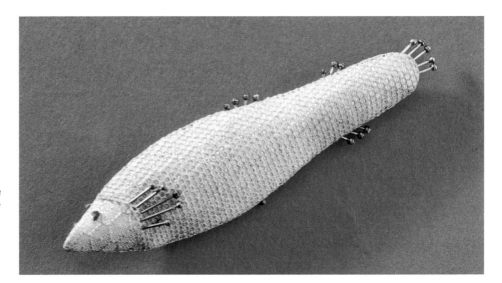

Colour Plate 66. Silk pincushion in the shape of a fish. An overlay of fine hand-made net creates the impression of scales and early original pins are positioned to form fins and a tail. c.1800. Length 2½in. (6.4cm.)

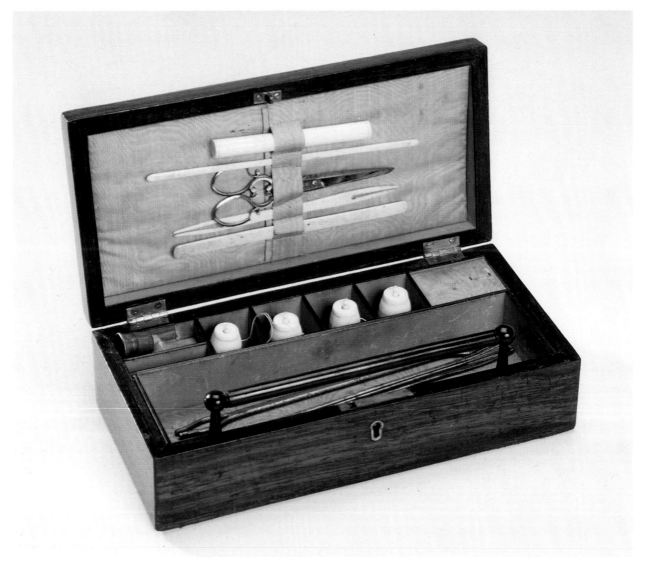

Colour Plate 68. Netting box and netting accessories. This box is fitted with the two major requirements of a netting box – a base that is weighted with lead to give stability and a roller in the front of the box that lifts up for use when netting. c.1800. Width 10in. (25.4cm.)

One of the most ancient crafts is the craft of netting. The making of nets dates back into antiquity when nets were essential for catching fish or trapping birds. What is interesting is that the same type of simple netting needle has been used for centuries, whether for fine netting for elegant gowns or for making camouflage nets during World War II. Netting needles vary in size and for hammock-making a needle of about two inches (5.2 cm.) wide would be used with thick cord but needles only one eighth of an inch (0.3 cm.) in width are used for fine delicate netting. Fishermen, sailors, fowlers, hunters, farmers and housewives all needed nets as they were constantly required for catching fish, trapping birds, penning poultry, storing vegetables and protecting fruit trees from birds. Netting, however, as a gentle craft, was at its height of popularity amongst the upper social levels of society during the Georgian era. It was thought to be quite acceptable for a man to net of an evening in the drawing room. The nets produced by men were usually used for covering fruit trees or catching birds.

Some exquisite fine examples of netting produced by ladies have survived and the fish pincushion (Colour Plate 66) has a fine overlay of net to give the effect of scales. A ball dress is illustrated in the March, 1810 edition of *Ackermann's Repository of Arts* (Colour Plate 67). This ball dress has a net coat over the dress that creates a delightful delicate effect.

When netting it is necessary to secure the initial loop to an immovable object. This can be a weighted pincushion, a hook that forms part of a clamp that can be attached to a table, a netting stirrup or a roller that is part of a sewing box or box specifically designed for netting. Netting boxes are usually utilitarian and Colour Plate 68 shows a typical example. The roller at the front of the box lifts up when used for netting. A layer of lead in the base of a netting box gives it weight so that the box will not move when in use and this is its most important feature. At the back of the netting box are sections for cotton barrels and a needlebook. A thimble fits into its own recess and the back right-hand corner has been fitted with a pincushion. The interior of the lid has been fitted to hold various tools required when netting.

There are two specific tools used for netting – netting needles and meshes. They both come in a variety of lengths and widths depending on the gauge of net required. Meshes – also called mesh sticks or gauges – are flat ruler-like lengths of bone, wood or ivory and are used to hold the loops

Colour Plate 67. Fashion Plate: 'Ball Dress'. A coat made of net gives a delightful delicate finish to this ball dress. From Ackermann's Repository, *March, 1810.*

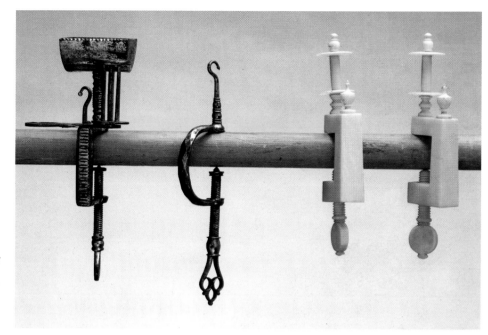

*Colour Plate 69. Left to right:-
Steel clamp with netting hook as
well as thimble holder, winding
cage and trough that was originally
fitted with a pincushion; steel
netting clamp; pair of ivory clamps
for winding and netting. Early
19th century. Length of ivory
clamps 4½in. (11.5cm.)*

*Colour Plate 70. Netting stirrup
made from black velvet and silk
ribbon and decorated with ribbon
embroidery. The sketch (Plate 8)
shows clearly how a netting stirrup
was used. Mid 19th century.
Length of embroidered velvet
6¾in. (17.2cm.)*

of thread. Netting needles, made from bone, ivory, wood or steel, are open at
each end and the thread is wound onto the needle lengthwise. Some examples of
netting needles can be seen in Colour Plate 68 with the netting box.

Clamps that were made purely for netting are usually made from steel although

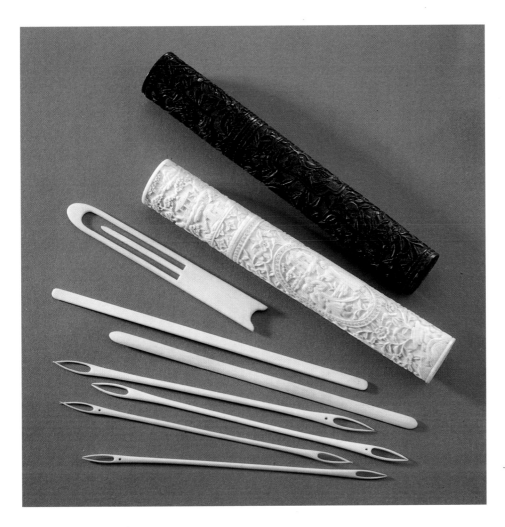

Colour Plate 71. Carved tortoiseshell and carved ivory netting cases made in Canton for the European market. The ivory netting pieces shown are typical fittings. Length of tortoiseshell case 6¼in. (16cm.)

a netting hook is often found on clamps of steel or ivory designed primarily for winding silk. The steel clamp, second from the left in Colour Plate 69, is the only clamp in this group designed purely for netting. The other steel clamp, as well as having a netting hook, has a ring to hold a thimble, a revolving cage for winding thread and a steel trough originally fitted with a pincushion but now unfortunately missing. The pair of ivory clamps both have posts at the front for netting as well as reels for winding thread.

A netting stirrup slipped onto a foot was an alternative method of holding the netting taut, and, because netting stirrups are made of fabric, few have survived. The black velvet and silk ribbon netting stirrup (Colour Plate 70) has been decorated with ribbon embroidery and, although this example is definitely not Georgian but rather from the Victorian era, it is useful to make a comparison with the sketch in Plate 8 that clearly shows how a netting stirrup was used.

Fine netting tools were kept in exquisite containers (Colour Plate 71) and these cylindrical containers are far more collectable than the tools. An enormous number made from ivory were carved in Canton for the European market. The tools they contained were sometimes faulty as the craftsmen carving them did not fully appreciate their working function. Often the V-shaped ends of the needles

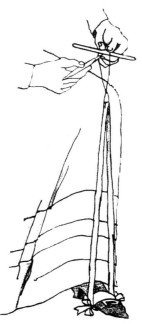

Plate 8. Sketch showing the method of using a netting stirrup (Colour Plate 70). The foot slips between a firm base and the embroidered velvet section and the top of the ribbon near the knee is used to hold the foundation loop.

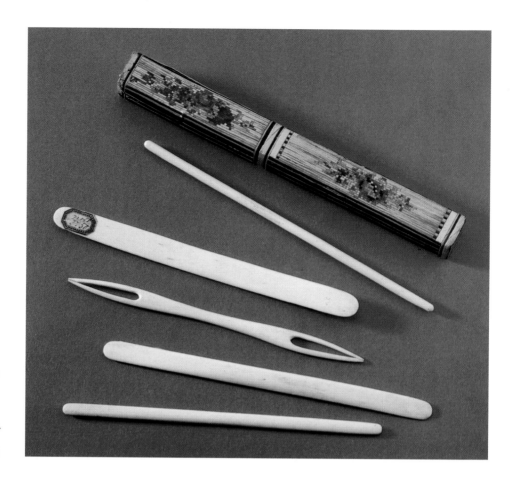

Colour Plate 72. Straw-work netting case and original fittings of meshes and netting needle. This case is a fine example of straw-work and the retailer's label is still on one of the meshes. English. Early 19th century. Length of case 6¾in. (17.2cm.)

are closed and consequently thread cannot be wound lengthwise along them. Straw-work containers were made in England to hold sets of netting needles and the illustrated example still holds its original contents with a retailer's label clearly seen on one end of a mesh (Colour Plate 72).

The making of cord up until the end of the eighteenthth century was a necessary occupation for all levels of society. Machine-made cord then came onto the market and, as it was quite affordable, this time consuming craft was dropped. Cord can be made in numerous ways, even by using the thumb and first finger of the left hand, but during the eighteenth century a lucet was the most usual cord making tool. A lucet (Colour Plate 73) can be made from mother-of-pearl, ivory, horn, bone or wood but is such a simple device the majority would have been made of fruit wood by villagers.

Instructions for using a lucet are as follows:-

1. Hold lucet in left hand with one end of thread through hole from back to front and hold thread down in front of lucet with left thumb.

2. With right hand bring thread up from back between forks and pass in front of and around right hand fork, then in front of and around left hand fork and in front of and around right hand fork again – this forms a figure eight around the two forks.

3. Hold thread between third and fourth fingers of left hand under slight tension at back of lucet.

4. With right hand loosen lower loop on the right prong and lift over the tip of the fork leaving upper loop on the fork.

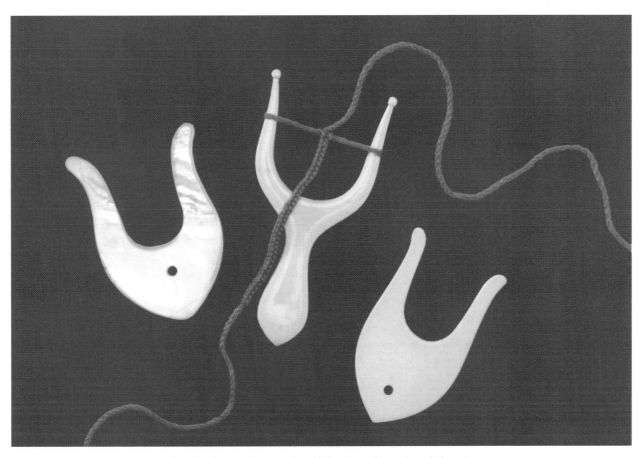

Colour Plate 73. Lucets of mother-of-pearl and ivory. A strong four-sided cord, as shown, is made by using a lucet. It is quite rare for a lucet to have a handle. Late 18th century. Length of lucet with handle 4¾in. (12.1cm.)

5.   Turn lucet around clockwise so back of lucet is now at the front.

6.   Pull thread tight towards the right with right hand.

7.   Pass thread round right hand fork. Continue steps 4 to 7 as above until cord is required length.

8.   To finish off remove cord from lucet and thread end first through left loop and then through right loop and pull tight.

The cord made by using a lucet is four sided and very firm. A vast number of clothes were held closed by lacing cord through eyelet holes and a firm cord was an absolute necessity. The diameter of the cord is determined by the thickness of the initial thread used.

Tambouring was another distinctive Georgian craft although it did have revivals in the Victorian era. A tambour hook is very similar to a crochet hook but the hooked end is sharp so that it easily pierces fabric. Usually the hook is held secure in the handle by a wing-nut and the angle of the wing-nut in relation to the angle of the hook does help when tambouring. Tambouring is a surface embroidery worked on fabric over a frame that originated in the East where the frame used resembled a tambour or drum. When tambouring the thread is held by the left hand under the frame. The tambour hook is pushed through the fabric on the frame, picks up the thread and draws a loop up onto the surface of the fabric. The next time the tambour hook is pushed through the fabric it is pushed through the

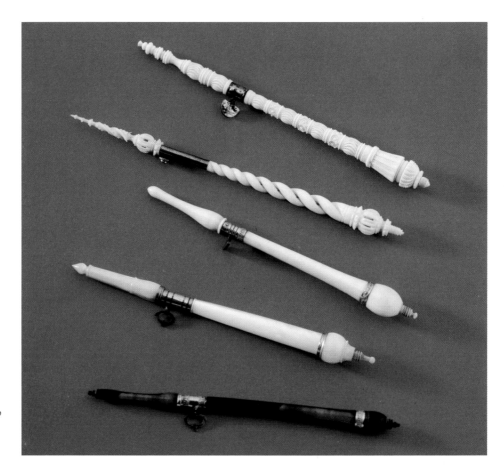

Colour Plate 74. Tambour hooks. The top three examples are of ivory – the first is the usual carved ivory variety, the second a rare intricately carved example and the third is the usual plain ivory type that is frequently found. A mother-of-pearl tambour hook (possibly from a Palais Royal box) and a rare tortoiseshell example are also shown. Early 19th century. Length of tortoiseshell example 4¾in. (12.1cm.)

preceding loop, thus creating a firm chain of stitches. After practice one becomes so proficient a series of chain stitches can be achieved much faster than using a needle and thread. Tambouring can be used for outlining or completely filling a whole design.

Like knotting, tambouring lent itself to an elegant pose and attractive affectations. Beautifully gowned ladies from the upper level of society used glorious tambour hooks while appearing to be busily occupied with this craft. Tambour hooks (Colour Plate 74) during the Georgian era were made from mother-of-pearl, tortoiseshell or ivory. Some of the ivory examples are plain with possibly a gold band – others are intricately carved. The end of the handle of these Georgian tambour hooks unscrews to reveal a cavity to hold spare needles. The covering of the needle when not in use screws onto the end of the handle thus lengthening the tambour hook. As strange as it may seem this additional length gives more dexterity when working.

Pin-balls were finely knitted with various patterns, often dated and sometimes initialled. These pin-balls were made in two parts and joined at the circumference. The wool filling was firmly packed and either a ribbon or cord used to cover the join. A long length of this ribbon or cord was left attached to the pin-ball so that it could be attached to the belt. Included with the examples of pin-balls in Colour Plate 75 is another pincushion knitted in fine silk. One side of this pincushion has a swan and tree knitted into the pattern while around the edge a message has been knitted that reads 'A Trifle from the Retreat 1819'.

A most interesting silk pincushion (Colour Plates 76 & 77) has been made in the form of a watch. One side has a painted watch face edged with fine blue

Colour Plate 75. Knitted pin-balls, one with a ship motif and dated 1798; one dated 1736 with metallic thread; one initialled EP and dated 1792. Knitted pincushion with a pattern of flowers, a swan and the message 'A Trifle from the Retreat 1819'. Diameter of pincushion 1¾in. (4.5cm.)

beads. The other side has the same beaded edging and a most attractive beaded centre. Gold thread has been used for the loop and 'chain' and the original pins with their separate heads are still intact. What is most interesting about this pincushion is the similarity to watches seen on macaroni chatelaines of the late

Colour Plate 76. Silk pincushion in the form of a watch with painted watch face and edged with blue beads. The ring and chain are made from gold thread. The pincushion has its original pins that were made with separate heads. c.1800.

Colour Plate 77. The reverse of watch pincushion shown in Colour Plate 76. The blue beaded decorative effect of this pincushion is similar to watches seen on macaroni chatelaines of the late 18th century. Diameter 1¾in. (4.5cm.)

Colour Plate 78. Regency fabric chatelaine, possibly of Spitalfield silk, that could be suspended from the high waistline of an empire gown or carried in the hand. Suspended from the small purse are a needlecase, scissors' scabbard with steel scissors and a pincushion. c.1820. Length 9in. (22.8cm.)

Colour Plate 79. Silk needlebooks decorated with fish scale embroidery. Fish scales have been used as petals in a layered effect to form flowers. The right-hand example also has chenille embroidery. Early 19th century. Length of smallest 3¼in. (8.3cm.)

Colour Plate 80. Reverse of needlebooks shown in Colour Plate 79. The left-hand example has a decorative spray of lily of the valley·that has been created with fish scales. The right-hand example has the additional feature of ribbon embroidery and the variegated ribbon used is almost identical to that used on the cushion in Colour Plate 50. Tiny stitches have been used to make both these rare exquisite examples. Early 19th century.

eighteenth century. It is almost an exact copy of one such example to be seen in Colour Plate 74 of *Chatelaines – Utility to Glorious Extravagance.*

Fashion plates from the Regency period sometimes show ladies with reticules suspended from the high waist bands of their empire gowns. The exquisite fabric chatelaine (Colour Plate 78), that appears to be of Spitalfield silk, could have been worn in such a manner or carried in the hand. This chatelaine consists of a drawstring purse that would have been ideal to hold threads or a thimble. Suspended from this purse are a silk scabbard to hold scissors and a disc-shaped pincushion with matching needlecase. This chatelaine has probably been made from scraps of silk left over from a glorious gown and has been trimmed with silk ribbon bows.

There is great debate as to the age of fish scale embroidery. There are those who favour the Victorian era for these embroideries and those who feel they are from an earlier era. The two needlebooks illustrated in Colour Plates 79 & 80 are made of silk material and ribbon that is obviously from early in the nineteenth century. On both these needlebooks fish scales have been used to imitate the petals of a flower. The stitching is exquisitely fine and chenille has been incorporated into the design, another feature typical of the Georgian era. Although crafts that were popular during the Victorian era were enthusiastically published in magazines of the day, the author has been unable to find any mention or instructions for fish scale embroidery whilst researching this material, thus adding weight to her opinion that it comes from the Georgian era. Fish scales become soft and pliable when soaked in cold water and it is then quite easy to pierce them with a needle. When dry, overlapping fish scales can be sewn onto a background material in the form of petals of a flower.

Colour Plate 81. Silk pincushion with steel engraving commemorating the death of the Duke of York in 1827. The message on the back of this pincushion (see text) refers to him as the 'Soldier's Friend'. Diameter 2¼in. (5.8cm.)

Two important pincushions dating from c.1820-1830 (Colour Plates 81 & 82) are made from silk that has been printed from fine steel engraved plates. One of these pincushions commemorates the death of the Duke of York in 1827 and under his picture on one side is 'Pub^d. by H. Miller, 14 Paternoster Row'. The other side of the pincushion has been printed as follows:-

> 'His Royal Highness the Duke of York was born 16th. August 1763. In his official capacity as Commander in Chief His Royal Highness exercised the great powers vested in him with that wisdom and discretion which stamps a lustre upon his name: under his fostering care a race of Heroes have appeared, and the soldiers of Britain are at once the dread and admiration of the world: he was unwearied in works of private benevolence; many a soldier's tear has been wiped away, and many widows and orphans have had their sorrows alleviated by the kind exercise of his philanthropy; in a word he was the SOLDIER'S FRIEND. His Royal Highness after great suffering died the 5th. January 1827 in his 64th. Year.'

The second of these two Royal Commemorative pincushions is made from similar silk material. One side has the picture of King William IV and the other side shows Queen Adelaide. Queen Adelaide, exquisitely coiffured and gowned, is standing next to a crown on a pedestal and no doubt this pincushion dates from the year of their coronation. The two sides of both of these pincushions have been finely stitched together at the circumference. The pins still retained in the commemorative

Colour Plate 82. Silk pincushion with steel engraving of King William IV on one side and Queen Adelaide on the other. c.1830. Diameter 2in. (5.2cm.)

pincushion for the Duke of York are mourning pins. They are the usual early pins made with separate heads but in this case have been painted black.

Samplers remained an important embroidery exercise throughout the whole of the Georgian era and although most were the work of young girls the example in Colour Plate 83 was possibly an exception. The text of this sampler is as follows:-

MARY ANN COLLINS
Born. at. No. 41. Flagon. Row
On. the 17. Day. of. march and
Baptized. in. the. Parish. Curch
Of. St. Nicholas. Deptford. on
The. 30. Day. of. april. 1820

This sampler most likely would have been completed soon after the Baptismal date and was possibly worked by the mother of Mary Ann Collins. However, Averil Colby records one birth sampler that was possibly made by an aunt and another worked by Sarah Taylor who recorded her own birth in great detail when she was ten years old.

Whether it is a sampler worked by a young girl, a fine embroidery or a tiny silk pincushion, painstaking hours, often in poor light, must have been spent making these treasures. We are but caretakers for a short time and must preserve them, to be passed on for future generations.

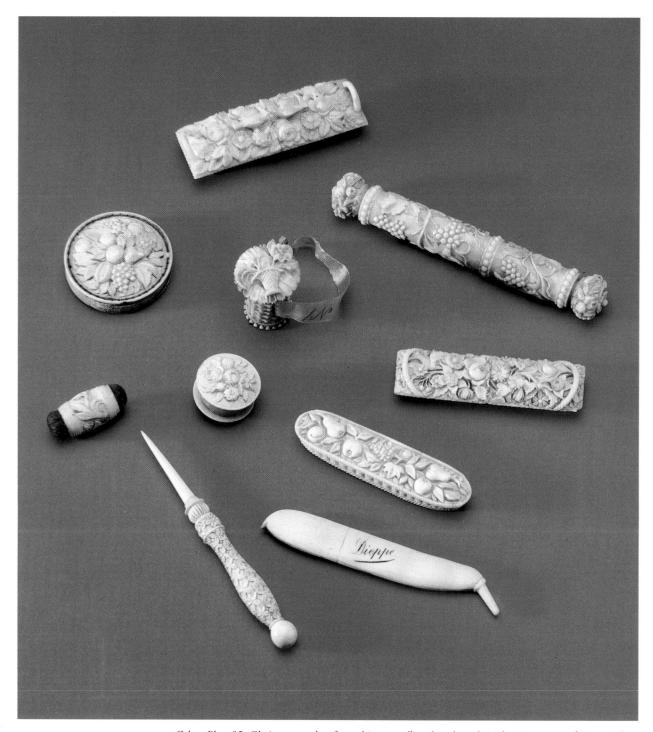

Colour Plate 85. Glorious examples of carved ivory needlework tools made in the Dieppe area of France. There are four needlecases – two in the shape of rectangular baskets of flowers, one with two doves, another with a decoration of fruit and the fourth is in the shape of a peapod and inscribed 'Dieppe'. The largest cylinder is a bodkin case and it and the needlecases all pull open near their centres. A tape-measure is in the centre of this colour plate, its silk ribbon marked in nails and its top a carved ivory basket of flowers. To the left of the tape-measure is a disc-shaped pincushion with a carving of fruit and the other disc-shape is a waxer. Also shown is a cylindrical emery cushion and a stiletto. Late 18th/early 19th century. Length of bodkin case 4¾in. (12.1cm.)

Chapter Six

Needlework Tools c.1750 to c.1840

The Era of Ivory

The most beautiful carved ivory needlework tools come from this period and it is interesting that they were at their peak of craftsmanship simultaneously in different countries around the world. The most exquisitely carved are French and come from the Dieppe area. Dieppe is a French seaport on the English Channel and as well as being the centre of ivory carving was a busy fishing port. The fisherfolk of Dieppe – both men and women – wore a distinctive traditional costume which is still worn today for special occasions. At the end of the eighteenth century and in the early nineteenth century small ivory figures were carved of fisherfolk wearing their traditional costume. These carved ivory figures opened at the waist and were containers for needles. A great amount of detail is carved on these figures (Colour Plate 84) and especially pleasing are the fish held in the hand and the lady's hand disappearing into the pocket of her skirt.

Pincushions, emery cushions, waxers, bodkin cases, needlecases, tape-measures and stilettos originating from Dieppe are quite distinctive (Colour Plate 85). The majority have a design of fruit and/or flowers carved onto their surface. Occasionally, the carving is in the form of baskets of flowers, birds or cherubs.

Colour Plate 84. Carved ivory Dieppe fisherfolk needlecases. These figures are wearing the distinctive traditional costume of this area of France. The needlecases pull open near the waist and needles are kept in the cylinder inside. Late 18th century. Height 3¼in. (8.3cm.)

The implements illustrated in this colour plate are typical of the quality of ivory carving from the Dieppe area.

Pincushions are made from two flat discs of carved ivory with a cushion in between. This has been attached firmly into place by stitching it around the circumference to both ivory discs. The pincushion featured has been carved on one side with a design of fruit and leaves.

Emery cushions were made in all shapes and sizes. Today we are familiar with emery paper and the grains of emery used in emery cushions is exactly the same product that is used on these sheets. Fine grains of emery are packed inside small fabric containers and are used to remove rust or sharpen pins and needles. It is quite easy to determine whether the cushion is a pincushion or an emery cushion. Apart from the weight – emery is much heavier than wool or sawdust filling – the grains of emery can be felt when a fine needle is pushed into the fabric.

Waxers were also constructed from two discs of carved ivory but have a central post between these discs that unscrews so that when required a new wax could be fitted between them. The waxer illustrated has flowers carved on one side and fruit on the other. When sewing, wax was used on the thread. By simply pulling thread along a piece of wax, a small amount adheres to the thread's surface and waxed thread slides through fabric, especially silk, very smoothly. It is interesting to note that wax is still used today for waxing thread in exactly the same manner, especially by quilters, even though commercially waxed thread is readily available.

Bodkin cases are just a larger version of a cylindrical needlecase. The exquisite carving on the illustrated example is of grapes and grape-vines. The bodkin case pulls apart towards the centre of the cylinder so that bodkins can be kept safely inside.

Two needlecases in this colour plate are exquisitely carved as baskets of flowers with handles at each end. The one at the rear of the colour plate has two doves, sitting amongst the flowers in the centre of the basket, on either side of the central opening. When the needlecase is opened a dove sits on each half and when closed the doves come together. The third needlecase has fruit finely carved along its top and again it has a central opening.

A beautiful basket of flowers has been carved on the top of the tape-measure, the cylinder of which is carved in the very popular basket weave design. The original silk tape is marked in nails.

The Dieppe ivory stiletto has a handle covered with carved flowers. The working section of the stiletto, when not in use, screws into the handle to protect the point. When employed, this working section screws into the handle with the point unprotected and ready for use. This was a very usual style of stiletto and the majority still have points in good condition as they could remain undamaged when not in use. A plain ivory stiletto achieves exactly the same function as one ornately carved. The point is used to push through fabric to make a hole, usually for eyelet work.

Another needlecase is featured in Colour Plate 85 and this example is an

Colour Plate 86. Ivory needlework tools with Shibayama decoration. Two peapod needlecases are decorated with the insects so typical of Shibayama. A tatting shuttle and disc-shaped pincushion have a Shibayama decoration of flowers. Early 19th century. Length of needlecases 3¼in. (8.3cm.)

incredibly accurately carved ivory peapod. When feeling these ivory peapod needlecases, as strange as it may sound, one can almost feel the peas within the pod. The peapod pulls open at the centre and needles fit into the cylindrical space inside. It has always been thought that these peapod needlecases were English in origin, but this example has been inscribed 'Dieppe' on one side and no doubt it was originally sold as a souvenir from that region.

Two other ivory peapod needlecases (Colour Plate 86) are extremely interesting and rare. These needlecases have been decorated with Shibayama – a Japanese craft that is the extraneous decoration and inlay of mother-of-pearl, ivory, jade etc., usually in the form of insects, birds or flowers. The two peapod needlecases are beautifully decorated with insects (the ladybird is especially pleasing) and are fine examples of this craft. It is interesting to note the similarity of the carving of the two peapod needlecases decorated with Shibayama to the peapod needlecase inscribed 'Dieppe'. The pincushion has also been decorated with Shibayama – the leaves coloured to contrast with the central mother-of-pearl flower. The tatting shuttle has a similar decoration of Shibayama. Although countless buttons and counters are to be found decorated with Shibayama this is not the case with needlework tools and only a small number are to be found in collections around the world.

The Chinese carving of ivory was centred around the busy port of Canton. It was here that merchants sold to American and European buyers. The style of

Colour Plate 87. Carved ivory needlework tools made in Canton with the typical deep carving of Chinese figures, trees and scenes. Back to front:- pincushion clamps (large and small) and winding clamp; two cotton barrels; needlecase; shuttle and silk winder. Early 19th century. Length of needlecase 3½in. (9cm.)

carving is quite distinctive and totally different from any ivory carving of European origin. The majority of pieces are carved with Chinese landscape scenes although a few implements, especially pincushions, have a grape leaf pattern. The landscape scenes usually include Chinese figures and the depth of carving and three dimensional effect is quite incredible. A great range of Chinese carved ivory implements can be collected (Colour Plate 87) — the quality of workmanship varying tremendously.

Clamps were produced in great quantities. One has a pincushion and is a most convenient aid when attached to the edge of the table. Winding clamps were used in pairs and were attached to the edge of a table at a distance apart necessary to hold a skein of silk firmly around both reels.

Cylindrical needlecases, netting cases, shuttles, pincushions, winders, cotton barrels — all were carved in this distinctive style. The Chinese craftsmen were skilled in their art. They excelled at carving any type of ivory box but were defeated, however, by their lack of knowledge of the practicality of some needlework tools. Thus, one occasionally finds a cotton barrel without a hole in the side and consequently the thread wound around the central spindle cannot be pulled out of the barrel. As previously mentioned, netting needles are often found with ends still joined so that thread cannot be wound along their length and shuttles that are delightful works of art but are totally impracticable.

The ivory needlework tools produced by English artisans are again quite distinctive (Colour Plate 88). An understanding of the use of the tools by these craftsmen meant they were extremely practical. Cotton barrels differed in size tremendously but all have spindles that turn smoothly and occasionally the spindle has a 'crank-handle' at the top. Thread can be pulled from the barrel through the hole in the side.

The plain cylindrical needlecase illustrated has great beauty by the addition of a carved crown as its finial. Another needlecase is in the shape of a key, that pulls open, so that needles can be stored inside.

Fretwork is distinctively English and beautiful pincushions were made in this manner. Two typical examples are illustrated in Colour Plate 89 both being made from discs of fretted ivory. The pincushion (left rear) has a long ribbon so that it could be attached to the belt. One standing pincushion has been combined with a tape-measure and the original silk tape, marked in inches, is branded 'London'.

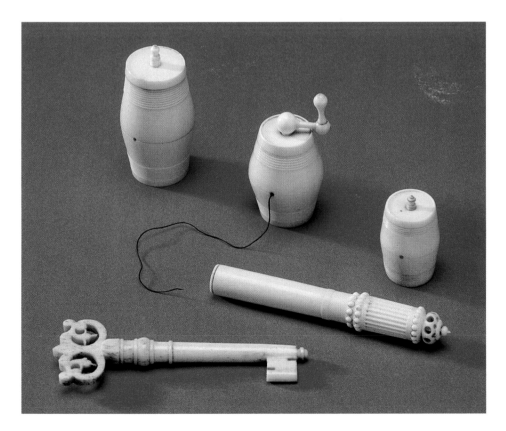

Colour Plate 88. Ivory needlework tools of a more restrained style produced by English artisans. The three cotton barrels were practical containers. One needlecase has a crown finial, the other is in the shape of a key and both unscrew at the centre. Early 19th century. Length of key needle-case 3¼in. (8.3cm.)

Colour Plate 89. Ivory fretwork needlework tools (English). Back row:- disc-shaped pincushion with ribbon for attaching to the belt, combination pincushion and tape-measure (original silk tape marked in inches) and pincushion in the shape of Stephenson's Rocket. Front row:- pincushions in the shape of a violin and a church and an ivory fretwork flat pincushion. Early 19th century. Length of violin 3¼in. (8.3cm.)

Miniature pierced ivory pincushions were produced in numerous shapes – some as simple as a leaf, some as complex as a violin or a church. The most complex of these fretwork pincushions is one made to commemorate Stephenson's 'Rocket'. The fineness of detail is exquisite – the wheels turn smoothly and the pincushion lifts up so that needles can be stored underneath. In England, as the Liverpool and Manchester railway line approached completion, there was a great deal of discussion as to the variety of engine that would be used for this new line. This led to the famous Rainhill Competition that was won in October, 1829 by George Stephenson with his steam locomotive called 'The Rocket'. The publicity that followed this popular choice even extended to the publication of an amusing caricature by G. Cruikshank that depicted travellers 'exploding' from 'The

Colour Plate 90. Ivory needlework tools decorated with black or navy-blue circles, dots and lines and now known as 'hot needle decoration', 'madras work' or 'dot and circle decoration'. Back row:- pincushion clamp, needlebook, tape-measure and clamp for netting and winding. Centre:- two disc-shaped pincushions one inscribed 'A Present from Beaford'. Front row:- silk winder, waxer, stiletto and two needlecases, one with a perpetual calendar and a seal base. English. Early 19th century. Length of stiletto 3in. (7.7cm.)

Rocket'. The most interesting and informative feature about this caricature is the similarity of the engine portrayed to the actual ivory pincushion.

Ivory needlework tools were produced in England with a distinctive decoration of black or navy-blue, circles, dots and lines. This decoration is similar to the decoration seen on Indian ivory sewing boxes and is discussed in full in Chapter 3. No doubt this method of Lac decoration originated in India and was then copied by English craftsmen. A great variety of needlework tools can be found decorated in this manner (Colour Plate 90) and it has become known as 'hot needle decoration', 'madras work' or 'dot and circle decoration'. The rarest of the illustrated examples is a needlecase with a seal base that turns to facilitate the

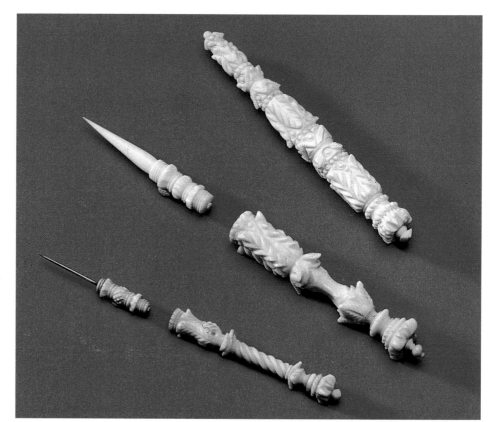

Colour Plate 91. Carved ivory needlework tools, thought to be of Indian origin. A lace pricker, stiletto and needlecase. The points of both the lace pricker and the stiletto screw into the handle for use. When not in use, however, they can be reversed and screwed into the handle to protect the points. Early 19th century. Length of needlecase 3½in. (9cm.)

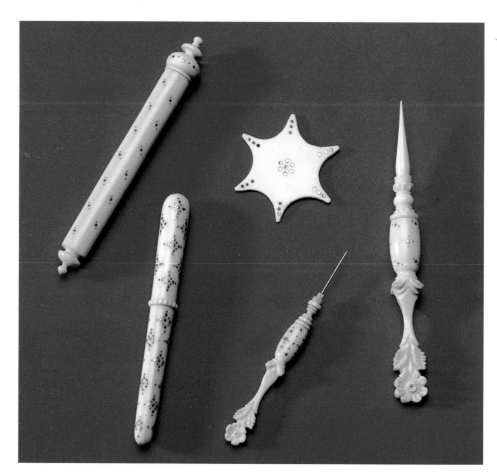

Colour Plate 92. Ivory needlework tools with piqué decoration. Left to right:- bodkin case, needlecase, silk winder, lace pricker and stiletto. Four of these tools are in excellent condition and still retain all their silver inlay, however, the winder has a considerable quantity missing. English. Early 19th century. Length of bodkin case 4¼in. (10.9cm.)

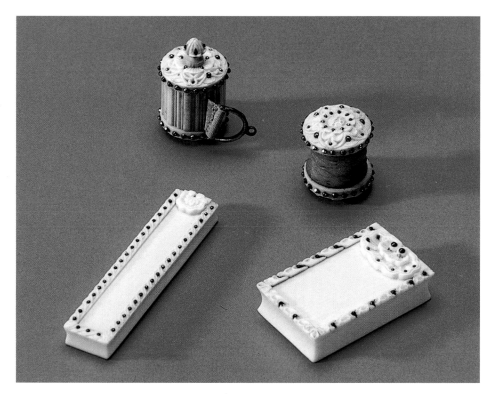

Colour Plate 93. Ivory needlework tools with clouté decoration. The word clouté comes from the French word meaning 'studded' and small pieces of steel 'nails' have been used to create this studded effect. The tools are :- tape-measure, waxer and two needlecases. Early 19th century. Length of needlecase on left 3in. (7.7cm.)

perpetual calendar. One of the pincushions has an inscription 'A Present from Beaford'. Beaford is situated on the Torridge River in Devon and was large enough to have its own souvenirs during the Georgian era. Also illustrated in this colour plate are two ivory clamps – one is fitted with a pincushion and the other is for netting and winding. A needlebook and tape-measure still have their original silk ribbons and a waxer has been made with wax between two discs of decorated ivory. A plain cylindrical needlecase matches the stiletto that unscrews so that the point can be reversed and screwed into the handle for protection. A delightful winder for holding silk thread completes this group of needlework tools.

The three ivory needlework tools (Colour Plate 91) are thought to be of Indian origin and illustrate another variety of ivory carving. The finial on the needlecase has been carved as a crown and matches the finials on the stiletto and lace pricker. This plate clearly shows how the points of the stiletto and lace pricker unscrew so that they can be reversed when not in use, thus protecting the point.

English ivory tools were also decorated with a fine inlay of silver that is known as piqué decoration. This fine inlay is quite exquisite and was used on a variety of needlework tools (Colour Plate 92). The needlecase illustrated has been heavily decorated with piqué in direct contrast to the bodkin case with its restrained amount of inlay. The lace pricker and the stiletto unscrew at the centre so that the working points can be screwed into the handles for protection. Silk winders with piqué decoration are quite rare and the workmanship of the illustrated example is not as fine as the other implements in this colour plate.

Not to be confused with piqué is the rarer form of French decoration known as clouté. The word clouté comes from the French word meaning 'studded' and is a much heavier decoration than piqué. To create clouté decoration, small pieces of steel 'nails' are hammered into the ivory surface creating a 'studded' effect – hence the use of the French word clouté. Ivory needlework tools with clouté decoration are illustrated in Colour Plate 93. The waxer and tape-measure are

Colour Plate 94. Sterling silver needlework tools. Back row:- two cotton barrels and matching winding clamp, two standing lady figural needlecases, set of three tools (emery cushion, waxer and tape-measure). Centre:- acorn-shaped tape-measure and silk winder. Front:- silk winder, lady figural needlecase, two needlecases (one made by Joseph Taylor and the other by Samuel Pemberton). Late 18th/early 19th century. Length of clamp 3¼in. (8.3cm.)

much heavier in style than other ivory needlework tools as it would only be possible to apply steel studs to a substantial base. Both of the two flat boxes have sliding lids and it is more than likely they were made originally as multi-purpose containers. However, identical types of containers are to be found with 'Needles' inscribed on the top. Boxes for toothpicks are similar but toothpick boxes usually have hinged lids with a mirror on the inside of the lid. Clouté decoration was also used on sewing tools made from wood.

Silver and Silver Filigree

Prestigious English silversmiths made needlecases at the end of the eighteenth century. These needlecases have bright cut decoration and usually have the maker's mark stamped on the base. The majority were made by Samuel Pemberton (SP) and Joseph Taylor (IT) but needlecases made by other makers are to be found. The rarest of these needlecases are fully hallmarked and two examples can be seen at the right front of Colour Plate 94. In the centre of this colour plate is a tape-measure in the shape of an acorn and, again, the sterling silver has a bright cut decoration. Bright cut sterling silver needlecases are

Colour Plate 95. Silver needlework tools with a decoration of silver wire and enamelling. These implements are of Chinese origin and each is inscribed 'MW to EM'. Left to right:- silk winder, stiletto, cotton barrel and pincushion. Early 19th century. Length of stiletto 3¼in. (8.3cm.)

frequently seen but it is difficult to find other matching needlework tools. There are three other needlecases in this colour plate (all known as figurals) and each has come from a European sewing set where 'the lady' fitted into a recess that was made to take the exact shape. Figural needlecases, especially the two standing examples, are extremely popular. On the left of this colour plate the two heavy sterling silver cotton barrels and matching clamp are heavily decorated with acanthus leaves and were probably made originally as part of a set for a Georgian box. The clamp would have originally been one of a pair for winding silk thread from a skein. It also has a post for netting. Three finely engraved matching tools on the right of this photo are an emery, waxer and tape-measure. An opening in the base of the emery reveals a cushion filled with grains of emery for sharpening pins and needles and removing any build-up of impurities. The tape-measure is marked in nails. These three needlework tools have no doubt come from a fitted sewing box as they have been made in the shape required to slot into place. The two silk winders illustrate the contrast in shapes to be found in silver examples.

Four other silver needlework tools (Colour Plate 95) are quite unique in style. Their decoration has been achieved with silver wire and part enamelling similar to cloisonné. Each piece is inscribed 'MW to EM' and, as they were purchased separately over an eighteen month period in the early 1980s, there are possibly matching pieces in other collections. When purchased, these pieces were thought to be Chinese in origin, but it was ten years later that this was confirmed by documents at the Peabody Museum, Salem, U.S.A. Articles at this Museum of similar workmanship have been dated to the early nineteenth century. These four needlework tools are a cotton barrel, pincushion, stiletto and silk winder, all with matching blue and green enamelling.

Needlework tools of silver filigree are mainly English in origin. Although some date from the middle of the eighteenth century, most date from the latter part of

Colour Plate 96. Silver filigree thimble case, combination thimble/needlecase and scissors' case. English. Mid 18th century. Length of scissors' case 3in. (7.7cm.)

Colour Plate 97. Silver filigree shuttle, needlebook and two bodkin cases. The needlebook has been fitted with flannel leaves to hold the needles. English. Late 18th/early 19th century. Length of shuttle 3¾in. (9.6cm.)

Colour Plate 98. Small silver filigree needlework tools. Rear:- two basket pincushions. Centre:- a thimble that holds the blue perfume bottle. Left-front:- a thimble. Centre-front:- a tape-measure. Right-front:- a combination tape-measure, thimble and perfume bottle (shown closed). English late 18th/early 19th century. Height of thimble 1in. (2.6cm.)

that century to early in the nineteenth century. Colour Plate 96 illustrates three of these early silver filigree tools. The shape of the separate thimble case and the one attached to the needlecase are exactly the correct shape for a silver filigree thimble made in the middle of the eighteenth century. The needlecase would have been less than satisfactory. The silver filigree scissors' case dates from the middle of the eighteenth century and, although fitted with scissors when purchased, these are of a later manufacture. It is rare to find scissors' cases with original scissors but the cases on their own are wonderfully collectable.

Four other silver filigree needlework tools are shown in Colour Plate 97. The silver filigree needlebook is highlighted with facets of silver that sparkle like diamonds. Silver filigree needlebooks with their flannel leaves were a far more practical holder for needles than a silver filigree cylindrical container. However, larger cylindrical containers were made from silver filigree for holding bodkins and two of these bodkin cases are also illustrated in this colour plate. Bodkins were still large until late in the eighteenth century when their size became smaller. Also featured in this colour plate is a silver filigree shuttle. It is difficult to find these shuttles in good condition as too much pressure on this fragile material when in use would have damaged the filigree.

Small implements of silver filigree (Colour Plate 98) are quite delightful and they must have been given and received with great pleasure in their day. The tiny basket pincushions are quite impractical for anyone involved in serious needlework and the thimbles, although knurled at the top for pushing a needle, must have been uncomfortably long even when used by Georgian ladies with slender fingers. The height of these silver filigree thimbles lent itself ideally to be

Colour Plate 99. Silver filigree bangle with silk holder. A ball of silk was held on the hook and the bangle worn on the arm when in use. German. Early 19th century. Length, including hook, 7½in. (19.1cm.)

Colour Plate 100. Silver filigree bangle silk holder. This example has a silver filigree ball to hold silk thread and the bangle is comfortable to wear on the arm when knitting, tatting or crocheting. German. Mid 19th century. Length 7½in. (19.1cm.)

fitted with a perfume bottle and in some cases a tape-measure as well. Thimbles used as containers for perfume bottles have a screw thread inside the base. Thimbles being sold on their own should not have this screw thread.

The silver filigree bangle silk holder (Colour Plate 99) has been stamped with an abundance of indecipherable marks. Although it appears to be of German origin it has an inscription in French dated 1833. Another variation of a silver filigree silk holder has a finely worked ball instead of a hook, to hold the ball of silk (Colour Plate 100). Again, it has a bangle to be worn comfortably on the arm. Bangles of this type were ideal for holding a ball of thread when working.

Early Painted Tunbridge Ware

Painted Tunbridge ware dates from the end of the eighteenth century and was made by craftsmen centred in Tunbridge Wells. Numerous needlework implements were included in the range of items produced and sold as souvenirs at Tunbridge Wells and fashionable resorts or spa towns such as Brighton or Bath. Small closed containers for holding pins known as pin-poppets (Colour Plate 101) were made of painted Tunbridge ware. The lids of these containers unscrewed or pulled off to reveal tiny cushions for pins. These containers were painted in a variety of ways, such as the one illustrated which resembles a beehive, another a speckled egg and the third has the traditional bands of colour painted

Colour Plate 101. Early painted Tunbridge ware needlework tools. Back row:- three pin-poppets – one in the shape of a beehive, another a speckled egg and the third, with ribbon that can be worn attached to the waist, is inscribed 'A Trifle from Brighton'. The small wooden pear is another tiny pin-poppet and each of these examples when opened have small cushions to hold pins that are protected by the lids. Also shown are two tape-measures – one in the shape of a castle, the other a house. Both have their original silk tapes marked in nails. English. Late 18th/early 19th century. Length of pear pin-poppet 2in. (5.2cm.)

on a sycamore container. This third example, with a label reading 'A Trifle from Brighton', has a long green ribbon attached to one side so that the precious pins could be kept safe hanging at one's waist. The fourth pin-poppet in this colour plate, although not of painted Tunbridge, needs to be included. It is a miniature treen pear that unscrews to reveal a tiny cushion still holding early pins.

Also featured in this colour plate are two painted tape-measures – one delightfully created as a miniature castle, the other a house. Both of these tape-measures have original silk tapes marked in nails.

Pincushion clamps made of painted Tunbridge were also popular and sometimes a tape-measure is fitted into the side of the clamp. The three illustrated in Colour Plate 102 are made of sycamore wood and have been decorated with bands of colour. Two are fitted with tape-measures, both marked in nails. One of the clamps is labelled 'A Bath Gift' the other 'A Token of Efteem'. Messages on early painted Tunbridge ware frequently make use of the long 's' (f). Tape-measures marked in 'Nails' (if original) do give an indication of their age and the author has found that all the early painted Tunbridge ware tape-measures she has examined have been marked in 'Nails'.

Colour Plate 102. Early painted Tunbridge ware pincushion clamps. The first is inscribed 'A Token of Efteem', the second 'A Bath Gift'. Spa towns sold these early Tunbridge tools as popular souvenir and gift items. Tape-measures are incorporated in two of these clamps, both with original silk tapes marked in nails. Late 18th/early 19th century. Length of clamp on left 4¾in. (12.1cm.)

Colour Plate 103. Multi-purpose clamp made in the Chinoiserie style with a tape-measure (marked in nails) in the shape of a house, beehive-shaped thimble holder and crown-shaped red velvet pincushion. The complete top section unscrews to reveal a cavity in the body of this clamp. Late 18th/early 19th century. Length 7in. (17.8cm.)

Colour Plate 104. Tortoiseshell needlework tools. Left:- a set of four reel holders and small cotton barrel. Right:- bodkin case, two needlecases one of which has a silver inlay of a bird and baskets of flowers and a silk winder. English. Examples shown are late 18th/early 19th century except set of reels which are c.1840. Length of bodkin case 5in. (12.7cm.)

An unusual clamp is featured in Colour Plate 103. This clamp has been painted in the Chinoiserie style and has three attachments on the top – a tape-measure, pincushion and thimble holder. The thimble holder unscrews at the centre and has been painted to represent a beehive in a similar manner to the pin-poppet previously discussed. The tape-measure is almost identical to the 'house' tape-measure featured in Colour Plate 101 and again its original silk tape is marked in nails. The complete top section of this clamp unscrews to reveal a cavity that was possibly used to hold pins and needles.

Tortoiseshell

Tortoiseshell was another material used late in the eighteenth century and early in the nineteenth century for needlework tools (Colour Plate 104). Its use, however, extended into the Victorian era, especially for veneering the exterior of boxes. Cotton barrels were thread holders of the Georgian era and it is most rare to find a tortoiseshell example. Equally rare is the tortoiseshell winder. Also featured in this colour plate are a tortoiseshell bodkin case and needlecase both with gold mounts and another tortoiseshell needlecase has a delightful decoration of silver inlay. Flowers in baskets, garlands, swags and urns are just some of the motifs used in this manner.

The tortoiseshell reel holders are from a later period of time to the small cotton barrel illustrated. The post attached to the base of these reels slots into the post

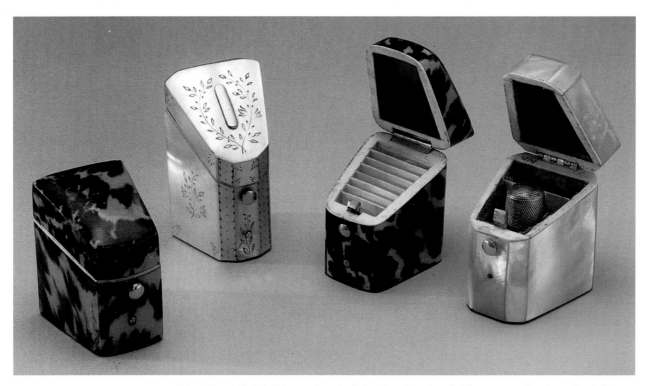

Colour Plate 105. Needleboxes of tortoiseshell and mother-of-pearl. The two examples shown closed illustrate the typical shape of these boxes and their similarity to the shape of a Georgian knife box. The open tortoiseshell box shows the ivory divisions to hold packets of needles in graduating sizes. The open mother-of-pearl example was made with a post to hold a thimble as well as packets of needles at the rear of the box. English. Height 2¼in. (5.8cm.)

attached to the top of the reel. When the top and the base are parted a reel or ball of thread can be put on the top post – the bottom section then fits back into place.

Needleboxes

The shape of the Georgian knife box was, without doubt, the inspiration for containers to hold packets of needles. It was early in the nineteenth century that needles first began to be sold in packets wrapped in a special paper to prevent rusting. Some of these early packets are extremely small, as the needles they held are fine and very tiny. Numerous packets of needles carry the inscription 'By appointment to her Royal Majesty Queen Victoria' – it is rare to find a packet that makes reference to William IV. Needleboxes were made of wood, veneered with mother-of-pearl or tortoiseshell and trimmed with ivory (Colour Plate 105). One of the mother-of-pearl needleboxes has been finely decorated with silver piqué. The interior of these boxes has a series of ivory divisions to accommodate packets of needles of graduating sizes. Some of these needleboxes have been made to hold packets of needles in a section at the back of the box – the front section being fitted with a post to hold a thimble.

Bodkins

During all periods of time bodkins have been an absolute necessity. Originally used for threading cord through eyelet holes for fastening clothing, they are still used today for inserting ribbon into lace edging on beautiful lingerie. Although still quite large during most of the eighteenth century, bodkins became smaller as

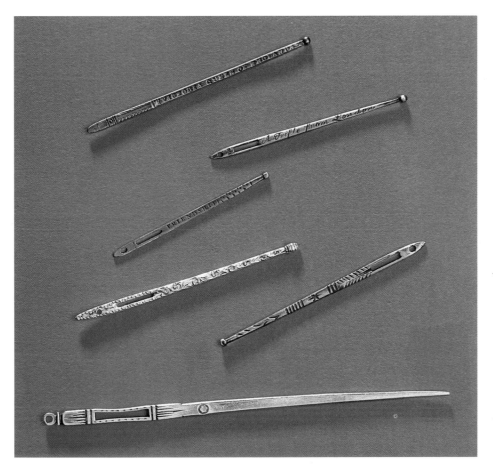

Colour Plate 106. A mid 18th century silver bodkin (at front) with five other bodkins that date from the late 18th and early 19th centuries. Back to front:- bodkin inscribed on one side 'Victoria, Queen of England' and on the other side 'Born May 24, 1819, Crown June 28, 1838'; steel bodkin inscribed 'A Trifle from London'; another steel bodkin 'Friendship without Intrest'; silver in the shape of a fish and a decorated steel fish bodkin. As a general rule the earlier bodkins are made of steel. English. Length of largest bodkin (mid 18th century) 4¼in. (10.9cm.)

the century drew to a close and those made early in the nineteenth century were no longer than 2¾ inches (7 cm.) in length. One early steel commemorative bodkin is inscribed 'Princess Charlotte died Nov. 6, 1817' while other small steel bodkins carry such inscriptions as 'Friendship without Intrest' (Interest spelt incorrectly) and another 'A Trifle from London'. Later bodkins were made of gilt metal – one popular example inscribed 'Victoria crowned June 28, 1838 Married to Albert Feb 10, 1840' was only 2¾ inches (7 cm.) in length. Other bodkins were made in silver – one popular variety being in the shape of a fish. A selection of bodkins are shown in Colour Plate 106 and, as a comparison of size, a mid eighteenth century silver bodkin has been included with a variety of examples dating from the end of the eighteenth until the middle of the nineteenth century.

Silk Winders

Although some winders have already been featured in this chapter, as they are such exquisite works of art they deserve further attention. The idea of winding thread onto a flat surface has been used for centuries, in fact, right up to the twentieth century. We all remember as children cutting cardboard into the shape of turrets of a castle and winding our threads onto these primitive holders. At the end of the eighteenth century winders were made from thin pieces of cardboard that were cut, either in the shape of a star, square or rectangle and edged with a fine strip of gold paper. They were used to hold fine silk embroidery thread that was purchased in skeins, and, with the aid of a pair of winding clamps, wound onto one of these silk winders.

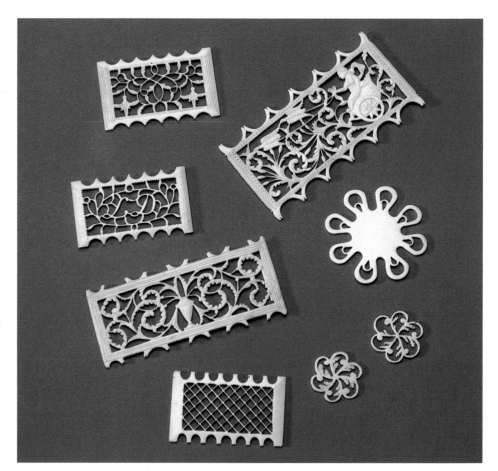

Colour Plate 107. Ivory fretwork winders are exquisite works of art. One has been made with initials worked into the pattern, one has been carved with a scene from mythology, while another achieves its beauty from a simple lattice pattern. The two small winders are known as snowflakes. Late 18th/early 19th century. Length of largest 3½in. (9cm.)

Colour Plate 108. Mother-of-pearl winders for silk thread. These examples show some of the enormous variety of patterns and designs available in this field for collectors. Shapes are as varied as the Maltese cross, four leaf clover or star. The three winders grouped top left of this plate are of Chinese origin and are engraved with figures and scenes. Early 19th century. Length of largest 3½in. (9cm.)

Colour Plate 109. Winders for silk thread were made from any suitable material. Back row:- straw-work, steel, blue glass. Middle:- two-colour glass in a butterfly shape, sandalwood, gilt metal. Front:- sandalwood, jasper, straw-work. 19th century. Diameter of largest 2½in. (6.4cm.)

Of all needlework tools, winders are possibly the most beautiful creations. It would be hard to find any other needlework tool to surpass the exquisite workmanship of the ivory winders featured in Colour Plate 107. When examining these winders one will delight at the beauty and workmanship of the fretwork, especially the lady in a chariot being pulled along by two doves and another where the initials 'LD' have been cleverly incorporated into the design. While not as elaborate, the winder at the bottom of this colour plate achieves its beauty through the simplicity of its lattice pattern.

The winders made for Palais Royal boxes (Colour Plate 44) are beautiful mother-of-pearl creations. Even though they are different, mother-of-pearl winders of Chinese and English origin (Colour Plate 108) are equally exquisite. The three winders top left corner of this colour plate are of Chinese origin and each winder has been finely engraved with an oriental scene that usually includes figures. The other winders show the enormous variety of shapes available – the smallest, for obvious reasons, are called 'snowflakes'.

The group of thread winders in Colour Plate 109 illustrate examples made of straw-work, steel, glass, sandalwood, gilt metal and jasperware. The steel, glass and jasperware winders are from the Victorian era but have been included here as a comparison of varieties. Winders of tartanware, mauchline and Tunbridge ware are also from the Victorian era and have been included in Chapter 9.

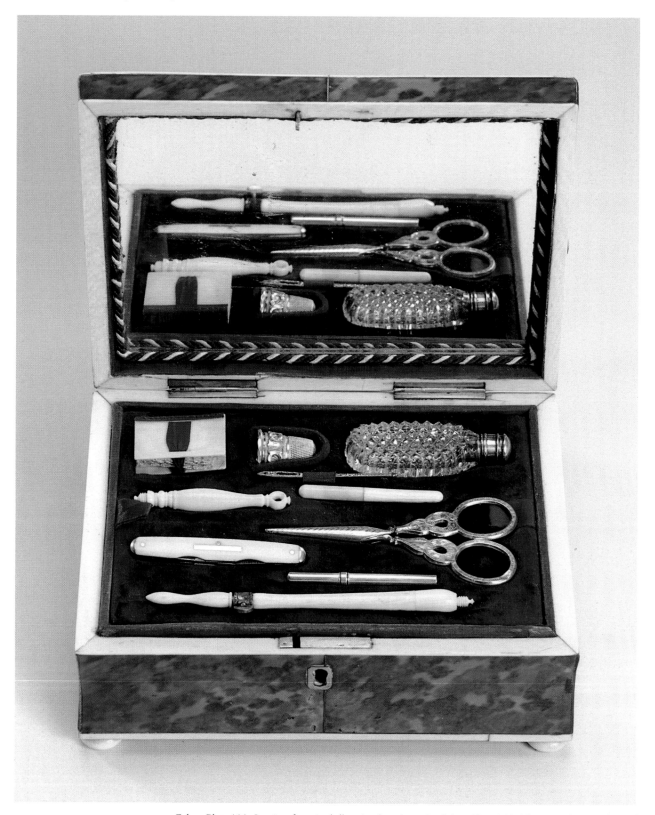

Colour Plate 111. Interior of tortoiseshell sewing box shown in Colour Plate 110. The mirror has an edging of blue and white cord, the tray and the interior of the box are lined in blue velvet and silk. Tools, predominantly ivory, fitted into the tray of this box are, back to front:- needlebook, thimble, perfume bottle, bodkin, needlecase, stiletto, scissors, knife, pencil and tambour hook. The interior of the box under the tray has been divided into compartments to hold cotton barrels. c.1820.

Chapter Seven
Nineteenth Century Sewing Boxes and Work Tables

Although Georgian sewing boxes continued to be made early in the nineteenth century it is the Regency period that produced another distinctive style. The tortoiseshell box (Colour Plates 110 & 111), with its domed top and bun feet, is typical of this era. The lid has a glorious inlay of mother-of-pearl flowers and leaves and fine strips of ivory have been used to give a finishing edge to the box. Thin pieces of tortoiseshell have been veneered onto a base frame to create this box. The tray has been fitted with some ivory and some sterling silver tools. It was at this period of time that ivory tools, in English sewing boxes, went out of favour to be replaced by beautifully carved mother-of-pearl. The space under the tray has also been divided into compartments for other embroidery requisites. The ivory stiletto in this box is one of the most popular varieties of stilettos used by needlewomen today as the point can be reversed and screwed into the handle when not in use. A ribbon could be fastened to the loop at the end of the handle of the stiletto so that it could be worn attached to the waist belt for convenience when being used constantly. These stilettos were made long before the invention of the stanhope peep view and 'peeps' were never fitted at the end of these handles.

Colour Plate 110. Tortoiseshell sewing box with ivory trim and typical bun feet. The lid has been decorated with a mother-of-pearl inlay of flowers. c.1820. Width 7in. (17.8cm.)

Colour Plate 112. Ebony sewing box with decorative mother-of-pearl inlay. This casket-shaped box has rings at each end for carrying and bun feet that are typical for this era. c.1830. Width 11in. (28cm.)

The ebony sewing box (Colour Plates 112 & 113) has been wonderfully decorated with an inlay of mother-of-pearl. It has the typical bun feet of the Regency period and rings are attached at each end of the box. The blue velvet interior is original and there is a folder inside the lid that flaps down when unclipped. This folder was used to hold paper patterns, possibly letters, in fact, any paper requisite. The tray that holds the mother-of-pearl needlework tools lifts out and the empty interior of the box could be used to hold small pieces of work in progress. The fittings in this box are original and matching. There are six mother-of-pearl reel holders and each of these reels holds a ball of original thread. There is a post attached to the base of these reel holders that slots into a post attached to the top of the reel. When the top and the base are parted a reel or ball of thread can be put onto the top post – the bottom section then fits into place. At the front of the box are three needlework implements with carved mother-of-pearl tops that match the carving on the mother-of-pearl reel holders. These three implements slot into round holes so that only the mother-of-pearl top is on view. The left-hand implement is an emery cushion and has a cylinder of bone underneath the mother-of-pearl top. There are holes in this bone cylinder that has been packed with fine grains of emery inside a material covering. Needles and pins can be pushed through the holes in the bone cylinder into the emery thus removing rust and sharpening the points. The middle implement is a tape-measure, in this case marked in inches, and the right-hand implement is a waxer. Waxers were used exactly as wax is used today by needlewomen. By pulling thread along the wax surface a small deposit of wax remains on the thread. Thread that has already been waxed is readily available today but some needlewomen, especially quilters, prefer to wax their thread themselves. On either side of the box in front of the reel holders are flat mother-of-pearl winders for holding silk thread. The variety of these mother-of-pearl winders is endless as can be seen in Colour Plate 108. There are three compartments with lids in the tray of this box

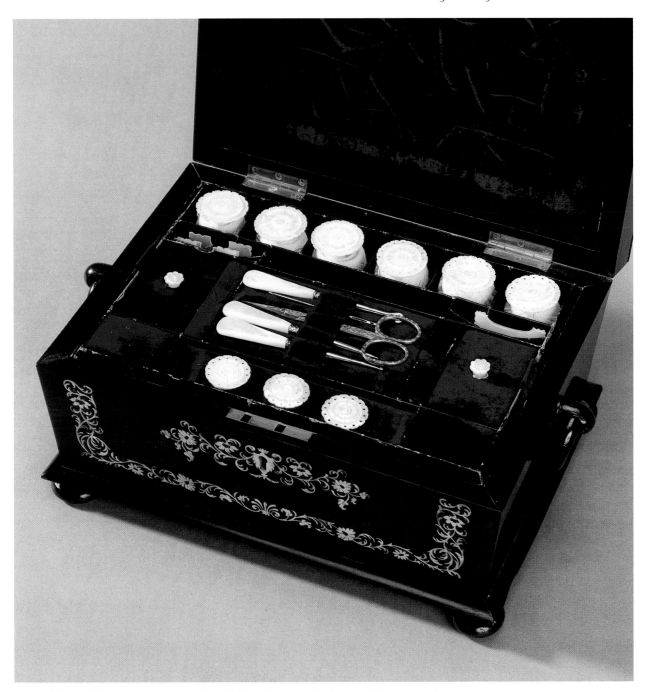

Colour Plate 113. Interior of ebony sewing box (Colour Plate 112) showing the rich blue velvet used to line the lid and the tray. An abundance of mother-of-pearl greets the eye when the box is opened. Mother-of-pearl needlework tools were now replacing the ivory examples found in earlier sewing boxes. The contents of the tray of this box are extensively discussed in the text. c.1830.

that could hold any number of small sewing requirements. The two outside lids have mother-of-pearl knobs for lifting while the centre lid has been fitted to hold button hook, bodkin, scissors, stiletto and crochet hook. On either side of these items are two blue velvet needlebooks that can be lifted out by the ribbon bows. These needlebooks are fitted with flannel leaves for needles. At the front of the box, on each side, are two built-in pincushions and recesses are provided to hold thimble and fingerguard.

Colour Plate 114. Casket-shaped sewing box with domed lid and bun feet. A glorious inlay of urns, stylised flowers and leaves has been achieved with mother-of-pearl and abalone shell while brass wire has been used for the graceful stems. c.1830.
Width 12in. (30.5cm.)

Colour Plate 115. Black lacquer sewing box with gold and red decoration. Handles are fitted at each end of this box for carrying. Although these boxes are quite common, because of extensive use and exposure to sunlight, few remain in good condition. Chinese. Early 19th century.
Width 11in. (28 cm.)

A similar domed sewing box can be seen in Colour Plate 114. A glorious inlay of urns, stylised flowers and leaves has been achieved with mother-of-pearl and abalone shell while brass wire has been used for the graceful stems. The interior of the box has been fitted with mother-of-pearl implements which are almost identical to the ebony box discussed previously.

From early in the nineteenth century lacquer needlework boxes were made in Canton for the European market. Black boxes with their distinctive gold lacquer

Colour Plate 116. Black lacquer sewing box extensively inlaid with coloured mother-of-pearl shell. Mid 19th century. Width 15½in. (39.5cm.)

work were frequently bought by traders and if requested the name of the recipient could be painted on the inside of the lid. These boxes are fitted with a netting ratchet and a multiple reel that are fixed within the box and removable individual tools such as cotton barrels, needlecases, clamps, winders etc. These needlework implements are made from bone or ivory and there is a tremendous variation in quality of workmanship. Some of the finest of these ivory implements are deeply carved with dragons, trees and people, in fact, a whole scene can be found on even the tiniest implement (see Colour Plate 87 and Chapter 6).

To produce a lacquer box was nothing new to Chinese craftsmen, however, they were often not informed as to the use of the individual tools and consequently, cotton barrels were made without a hole through which the thread could be drawn and netting needles were produced with an eye at each end that did not have an opening slit. The lacquer box in Colour Plate 115 is a fine example of Chinese craftsmanship. It still retains all of its gold lacquer work which on most boxes is very rubbed or faded.

Another style of black lacquer sewing box is illustrated in Colour Plate 116. This box is also of Chinese origin and was made for the European market. The exterior of the box, the inside of the lid and the covers of the interior compartments are beautifully inlaid with coloured mother-of-pearl shell. The interior of the box is unlined which is to be expected as lacquer boxes of this variety were never lined with paper or fabric.

Colour Plate 117. Small French Empire sewing box. Green paper covering edged in gold and lid decorated with gold paper gardening basket and beehive. Width 5½in. (14cm.)

Colour Plate 118. Interior of French Empire sewing box (Colour Plate 117) with its fittings mainly of paper or cardboard. The metal stiletto, bodkin and thimble were included in this box at the time of purchase but may not be original.

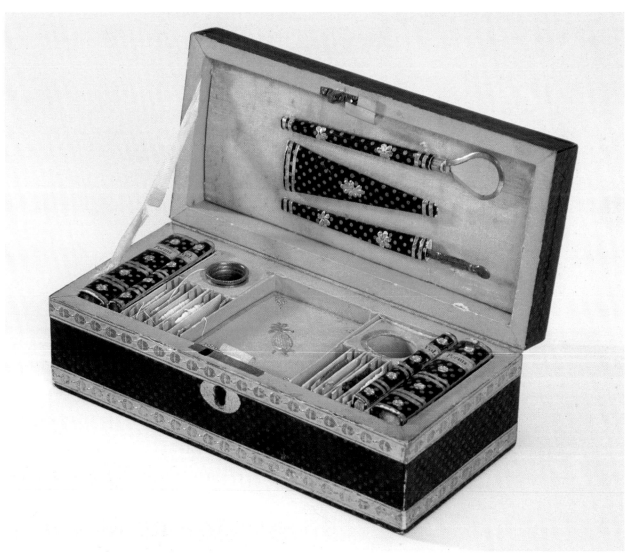

Colour Plate 119. Tunbridge ware boxes. Left:- cotton reels in graduating sizes are fitted into this box. Centre:- sewing box. Right:- pleat box with weighted base. A close resemblance can be seen in the decorative patterns of Tunbridge ware to the designs of Berlin woolwork (see Colour Plate 121). c.1840. Width of pleat box 4½in. (11.5cm.)

The sewing box in Colour Plates 117 & 118 is a great contrast to those already discussed. This box has a covering of paper and is typically from the French Empire period. A gardening basket and a beehive are featured on the top of the box and heavy paper and cardboard have been used for most of the fittings. Paper scabbards have been fitted to the flap inside the lid and these scabbards hold a stiletto and bodkin although unfortunately the scissors are missing. Two spaces are provided for thimbles but only one thimble is still in place. A central section is covered with a gold paper decorated cardboard lid. Four 'books' slide neatly into their allocated spaces – the two larger actually being pincushions. One of the little 'books' holds a silk tape-measure that has been wound around a piece of cardboard, the other opens up as a needlebook. There are nine cardboard winders (one missing), each with an edging of gold paper, the majority holding various coloured silk threads. Although this box shows evidence of use it must have been handled carefully as paper and cardboard would not be suitable for anyone heavy-handed.

A collector whilst looking for sewing boxes will find an endless variety of boxes made of Tunbridge ware. Tunbridge ware is the process of inlaying natural coloured woods in a mosaic or marquetry pattern. It originated in the area of Tunbridge Wells by craftsmen working in wood from the late 1820s. Tunbridge Wells, like all Spa Towns, proliferated in souvenir ware, although ironically the craft flourished as the interest in Spas declined. Tunbridge ware sewing boxes were made in different sizes and frequently the box was designed for a specific purpose. The box on the left in Colour Plate 119 has been designed to hold seven cotton reels in decreasing sizes. It has a marbled veneer with geometric mosaic inlay. The box on the right is a pleat box. The base of this box has been weighted with lead so it will not move when used to hold a pleat in place. A pincushion has been fitted into the hinged lid of the

Colour Plate 120. Tunbridge ware sewing box. The lid has been fitted with a pincushion. c.1840. Width 8¾in. (22.4cm.)

Colour Plate 122. Tunbridge ware sewing box – the lid featuring an inlay of the Prince of Wales Feathers. It is thought that this box was made to commemorate the birth of Queen Victoria's first son in 1841. The contents shown in front of the box are a rare set of Tunbridge ware reels, a tape-measure, combination pincushion/waxer and winder. It is most unusual to find tape-measures still being marked in nails this far into the 19th century but the silk tape is original. Width 9in. (22.8cm.)

Colour Plate 121. Berlin woolwork sampler. The obvious similarity between these designs and those featured on Tunbridge ware boxes is most interesting. c.1840. 9½ x 7½in. (24.2 x 19.1cm.)

box for convenience and the interior has been left empty to hold needles and threads. The mosaic patterned band around this pleat box is identical to the bands of mosaic on the small sewing box at the rear of the colour plate. The sewing box has been made with compartments to hold various needlework tools.

The Tunbridge ware box in Colour Plate 120 also has a pincushion fitted into the hinged lid and the decorative mosaic inlaid band around this box looks exactly like a Berlin woolwork embroidery. This form of embroidery was extremely popular in the 1840s and patterns were copied in wood mosaic. It is interesting to compare the patterns in the Berlin woolwork sampler (Colour Plate 121) to the Tunbridge boxes in this chapter. The similarities are very apparent.

The Tunbridge ware sewing box in Colour Plate 122 has a mosaic inlay of Prince of Wales feathers on the lid and is fitted with Tunbridge ware needlework tools. The five Tunbridge ware cotton reel holders are rarely found individually and a set is to be treasured. The tape-measure has its original tape marked in

Colour Plate 123. Walnut sewing box profusely decorated with an inlay of ivory. Rings are fitted at each end for carrying. From about this date sewing boxes were made without feet, the base having a green hessian covering. c.1840. Width 11in. (28cm.)

Colour Plate 124. Papier mâché sewing box made by Jennens & Bettridge. The lid features a painting of the Crystal Palace, Hyde Park with mother-of-pearl used to highlight the glass panels. Papier mâché was prominently displayed at this exhibition as it was then at the height of its popularity. c.1851. Width 10½in. (26.7cm.)

'Nails' and the waxer has been fitted with a pincushion – a combination often seen in Tunbridge ware pieces. Slots are provided in the box for a set of winders but only one of these rare Tunbridge examples still remains in place. Tunbridge ware needlework tools are further discussed in Chapter 9.

Although it was more usual for sewing boxes to have an inlay of mother-of-pearl, sometimes ivory was used in exactly the same manner and the sewing box in Colour Plate 123 shows this use to glorious effect. This walnut box dates from

Colour Plate 125. Coromandel sewing box made by Fisher, 188 Strand, and presented to Miss Boundy in 1875. This box still retains an amazing number of original mother-of-pearl reels. The mother-of-pearl lids on the four compartments are most unusual. The drawer has been fitted to hold jewellery. Width 12in. (30.5cm.)

c.1840 and from about this time boxes were made with flat bases – they had no feet. Usually the base of these boxes was covered with a green hessian and care must be taken to ensure that a box was not from an earlier era with the feet removed. There is always the possibility that a box with one foot missing has had the other three removed and fabric glued to the base to cover the evidence. Although this box was copiously decorated with ivory, it would have been fitted with mother-of-pearl sewing tools.

The Great Exhibition of the Industry of All Nations opened in May, 1851 at the Crystal Palace, Hyde Park, London. A great number of sewing boxes were produced for this exhibition with some made to commemorate the actual event. Papier mâché was at its height of popularity and the sewing box (Colour Plate 124) combines the high quality workmanship of Jennens & Bettridge with the event of the era. The painting of the Crystal Palace on the lid of this box comes to life by the use of mother-of-pearl for the glass panels.

It is rare to find a sewing box that has mother-of-pearl lids over the interior compartments but the Coromandel sewing box in Colour Plate 125 not only has such lids but an amazing number of matching mother-of-pearl reels. There are two hidden springs – one to release the mirror and another to open the drawer in the base of the box. A maker's plaque inside the box is inscribed 'Fisher, 188 Strand' and the lid of the box has been inscribed :-

Presented to
Miss Boundy
In grateful acknowledgment of her
Gratuitous services for several years
AS ORGANIST AT BETHANY
and afterwards at
ARGYLL CHAPEL
SWANSEA
15th July, 1875

Colour Plate 126. Rosewood sewing box with mother-of-pearl inlay even extending to the inner edge of the box. Sewing boxes similar to this example and Colour Plate 125 are difficult to date as they were a popular style for at least two decades. Width 12in. (30.5cm.)

The needlework tools shown in this box are original and include an unusual number of reels with mother-of-pearl tops. The set of eight reels are slightly larger than the set of five reels at the back of the box but all have a matching ridge around the edge of the mother-of-pearl. The steel stiletto has a handle of mother-of-pearl with a ridge at the edge of the mother-of-pearl that matches the reels. The only other tool in the box when it was purchased is a perfectly fitting silver needlecase that appears to be original.

Boxes similar in style to the one presented to Miss Boundy were popular for a considerable period of time. The dating on the plaque implies that the box, if given when new, was made during the 1870s but it would not be unusual for an almost identical box to have a provenance that dates it to more than a decade earlier.

The box illustrated in Colour Plate 126 also has documentation that implies it was from the 1870s. This Rosewood sewing box has been gloriously inlaid with mother-of-pearl and brass even to the extent of decorating the rosewood inner edge of the box that can be seen when the box is open. The maker's label is still intact under one of the compartment lids in the tray of the box and reads:-

AUSTIN
Manufacturer
7. St. Andrew St.
DUBLIN

This label and some delightful cards found in the box (Colour Plate 127) indicate that Susanna MacDonnell received the sewing box after she had been 'Examined for Confirmation March 19, 1877' and 'Admitted to the Holy Communion on 1st day of April, 1877'. Susanna's box, like Miss Boundy's, is of a style that was popular for decades and it is difficult to determine if it was new when given as a present in 1877.

Colour Plate 127. The maker's label 'Austin – Manufacturer – 7 St. Andrew St., Dublin' found under the lid of a compartment in the box shown in Colour Plate 126. Also found in this box are the cards showing that the box was given to Susanna MacDonnell in 1877.

A sewing box was not only used to hold a lady's needlework requirements. It was her private domain where a love letter, a pressed flower or a small momento could be stored away. Years ago most sewing boxes that came onto the market were full of wonderful treasures. As well as needlework implements there was an abundance of ribbons, laces, threads, buttons, cards, verses .... the list is endless. Sadly, today, it is rare to find those personal items and one can only hope they have been kept by the family. Often an article in a sewing box has no connection with needlework as the sewing box has been used for safe storage and consequently assumptions are incorrectly made about these articles.

The contents of sewing boxes are sometimes completely intriguing. In one Victorian box carefully prepared on a piece of cardboard was an assortment of needles, threads and buttons. Attached to this piece of cardboard was a card with the following verse:-

> 'Oh how I pity you poor desolate man,
> Others may laugh I wonder they can
> When rising up some cold frosty morn
> With buttonless shirt and stockings all torn
> No wonder then that you stamp, moan and fret
> These utensils I've sent till a wife you get.'

What prompted this home-made sewing kit? Was it sent by a mother to her son while he was a bachelor living away from home? One can only wonder.

A new owner of any sewing box has the choice as to whether a box remains exactly as it was when purchased or adds pieces to fill the empty compartments. Personally, I prefer to live with a box with missing pieces, but, if additions are made, hopefully they will be added sympathetically.

Colour Plate 128. Walnut work table with a central tapering drum to hold embroidery. Small compartments around this drum, under the lift-up lid, are ideal to hold needlework tools. c.1860. Height 28in. (71cm.)

Colour Plate 129. Mahogany work table. The interior has been fitted with compartments to hold embroidery and needlework tools. The style is similar to teapoys from the same era. c.1830. Height 30in. (76.2cm.)

Victorian ladies of quality kept their embroidery in a work table. These small pieces of furniture were made from the finest highly polished timber in a variety of styles. The most usual has an octagonal top with a lift-up lid (Colour Plate 128). The body of this walnut work table has compartments around a central tapering drum that has a tripod base. Quite often this style of work table had an additional use as the lid was inlaid as a games table. The compartments around the edge of the octagonal top were used for needlework or games requisites while the central drum was ideal to hold pieces of embroidery in progress.

Another work table of mahogany (Colour Plate 129) looks at first glance to be a teapoy but it has been fitted as a work table. When the lid is raised the matching mother-of-pearl fittings are revealed, each in its own compartment around the edge. The central section is ideal to hold work in progress. The inscription on the plaque under the key reads :-

Henrietta Bedford
A Present
from her Mother
1874

No doubt the inscription on this plaque was added long after the work table was made and often dated plaques are misleading as this work table dates from the William IV period.

The burr walnut work table (Colour Plate 130) has a drawer that slides out under the compartmented upper section. The drawer in this example is made of timber but frequently a fabric bag is fitted to the slides as this was ideal to hold embroidery. The upper compartmented section, under the lift-up lid, is large enough to hold the necessary needlework tools, a range of threads and a small selection of fabrics.

Papier-mâché work tables as well as papier-mâché sewing boxes (see Colour Plate 124) were featured at the Exhibition of All Nations (Crystal Palace) in 1851 and judging by the large number of these work tables seen today, they must have been very popular.

Lacquer work tables similar to the sewing box in Colour Plate 115 were imported from Canton to Europe and again these are frequently seen on the market. Unfortunately, exposure to sunlight has meant that most of these lacquer work tables have very faded lids.

It is important that the interior of work tables remains as original as possible and even if the paper lining has some slight damage it should not be replaced.

Towards the end of the nineteenth century sewing boxes and work tables went out of fashion to be replaced by sewing baskets and ladies' magazines were full of advertisements for silk lined baskets of various shapes. Most of these baskets had divisions, often on the inside of the lid, to accommodate a variety of needlework tools. Some baskets were on a stand and being light were portable, unlike the earlier wooden work tables. Although these sewing baskets were extremely functional they did not have the beauty and elegance of a sewing box and sadly these have never returned to fashion.

Colour Plate 130. Burr walnut work table with compartments for needlework implements under the lift-up lid.
The slide drawer is ideal for holding embroidery. c.1840. Height 27½in. (69.8cm.)

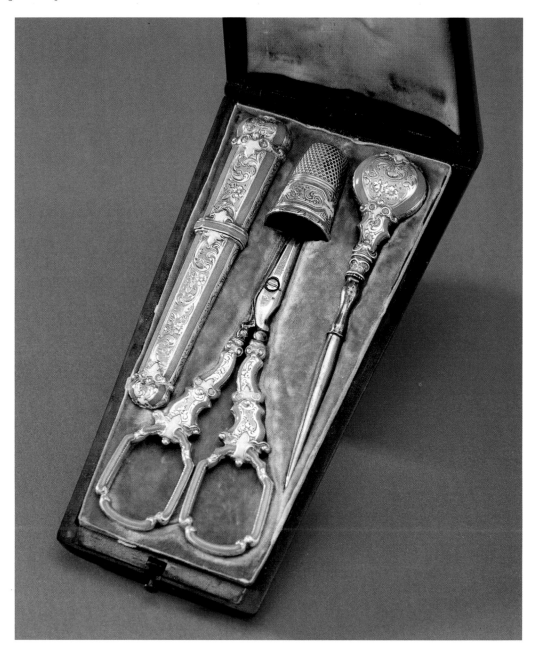

Colour Plate 133. French sewing set in tortoiseshell case retailed by Read & Son, London. The needlework tools are of gold, beautifully enamelled. A bodkin is included in this set and is inside the needlecase, something that is quite usual with French sewing sets. Each tool is marked with an eagle's head which is the Paris gold mark for 1838-1846. Length 4¾in. (12.1cm.)

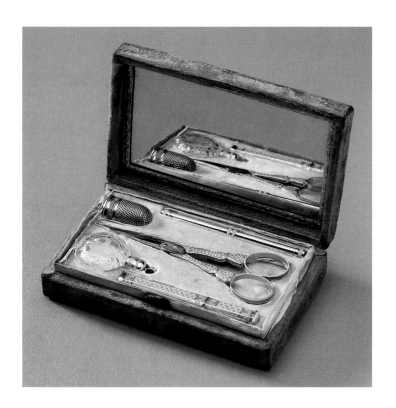

Chapter Eight

Nineteenth Century Sewing Sets

An abundance of sewing sets was made during the nineteenth century and although some of these are of English origin, the overwhelming majority are French. It is unfortunate that the French did not have a concise yearly system for marking silver, silver gilt or gold as their *petite garantie* marks cover lengthy periods of time.

The French gold sewing set (Colour Plate 131) is clearly marked on each piece with a cock's head which dates it for Paris 1809 - 1819. All the pieces are matching and original and the pencil within its gold holder has never been sharpened. Inside the needlecase is a matching bodkin. Bodkins are usually included in French sewing sets and, if there is no specific place for a bodkin, they are found inside the needlecase. The pieces in this set are pristine and show no evidence of use which is in direct contrast to the case which is worn and rubbed and appears to have been stored in a damp environment.

Another French gold sewing set is in a satinwood case (Colour Plate 132). All the pieces have a matching pattern and in this set the bodkin has its own specific place. Each implement is marked with a horse's head – Provinces after 1838.

Colour Plate 131. French gold sewing set. The fittings are a pencil, thimble, scissors, perfume bottle and needlecase. Each piece is marked with a cock's head for Paris 1809-1819. Box 4½ x 2¾in. (11.5 x 7cm.)

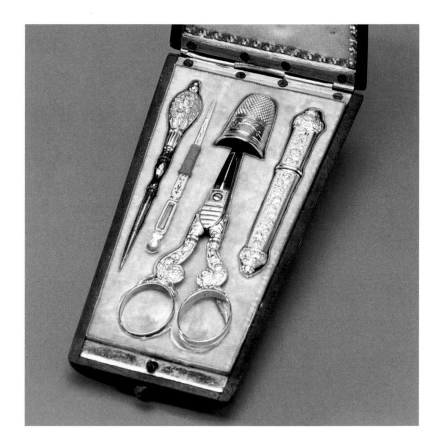

Colour Plate 132. French gold sewing set in a satinwood case. The fittings are a stiletto, bodkin, thimble, scissors and needlecase. Each piece is marked with a horse's head indicating the Provinces after 1838. Length 4¾in. (12.1cm.)

Colour Plate 134. A most popular sewing set of silver gilt that fits into recesses in a solid ivory case. This sewing set is comprised of a crochet hook, stiletto, bodkin, thimble, scissors and needlecase. Marked with a boar's head for Paris after 1838. Length 4½in.(11.5cm.)

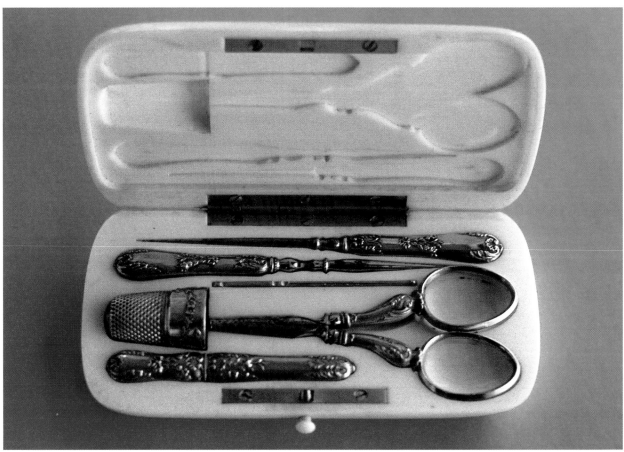

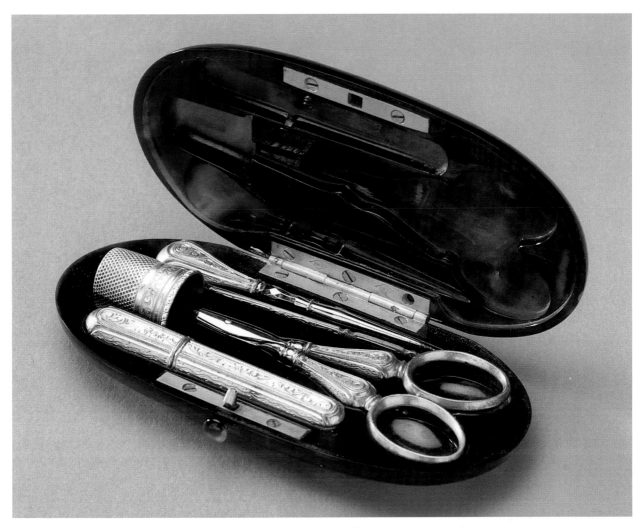

Colour Plate 135. Silver gilt sewing set fitted into recesses in a solid tortoiseshell case. Missing pieces in these sets are almost impossible to replace as the recesses were made to fit specific individual pieces. Marked with a boar's head for Paris after 1838. Length 4½in. (11.5cm.)

The sewing set in Colour Plate 133 is also of French origin but has been retailed by Read & Son, Jewellers, 77 Jermyn Street, London. This case is tortoiseshell and the pieces are beautifully enamelled gold. A matching enamelled bodkin is in the needlecase. This set is clearly marked with an eagle's head which is the Paris gold mark for 1838 - 1846.

Each of these three sewing sets has cases of different materials – plush, satinwood and tortoiseshell, but each tray that holds the needlework tools is of cream satin with recesses, sometimes edged with silk, that are made so that each tool fits perfectly into the recess.

Another type of French sewing set that was extremely popular had a case of solid tortoiseshell or ivory. Recesses were made in the solid base and lid of these cases to exactly accommodate the needlework tool. Found more frequently in ivory they usually have five implements – a stiletto, bodkin, thimble, scissors and needlecase, however, the example (Colour Plate 134) has a crochet hook in addition and some examples also have a pencil. The tortoiseshell example (Colour Plate 135) also has five implements and both of these sewing sets are silver gilt marked with a boar's head for Paris silver after 1838.

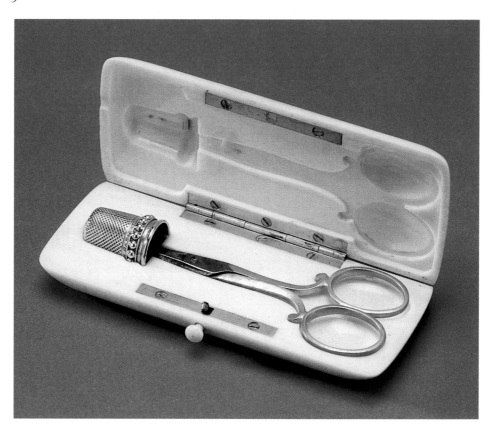

Colour Plate 136. Solid ivory case with recesses to hold a gold thimble and gold handled scissors. French c.1840. Length 4¼in. (10.9cm.)

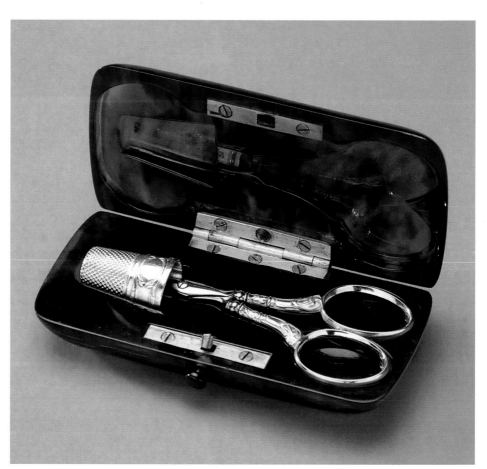

Colour Plate 137. Tortoiseshell case with recesses to hold a gold thimble and gold handled scissors. French. c.1840. Length 4½in. (11.5cm.)

Colour Plate 138. Spanish walnut lined with silk and fitted with a silver gilt frame that holds a miniature silver gilt sewing set and Bristol blue perfume bottle. French. Marked with a boar's head for Paris silver after 1838. Width 2in. (5.2cm.)

Two other sewing sets (Colour Plates 136 & 137) have cases made from ivory and tortoiseshell. Both of these sets only have two implements – a thimble and a pair of scissors. In both of these sets the thimble and the handles of the scissors are gold and, although sets containing five or more gold implements are found, it is more likely they will be silver gilt.

Collectors are frequently under the misapprehension that if these tortoiseshell or ivory sets have pieces missing they can be easily replaced. It is almost impossible to find needlework tools to fit exactly into the recesses that were made for specific pieces. French silver gilt needlework tools from this era are themselves difficult to find and an incomplete sewing set should never be purchased with the thought that it is easy to find replacement pieces.

While discussing French sewing sets the fitted walnut (Colour Plate 138) must be included. Although these sets are an absolute frivolity, each tiny tool is in first class working order. These large walnuts were grown in Spain, taken to Paris where they were lined with silk and fitted with a silver gilt frame that held a variety of tools. The tools in the illustrated example are (from back to front):- an ivory pad for writing notes, a pair of scissors (sharp enough to cut), a pencil, stiletto, bodkin, rule and nail file. On either side of the case is a thimble and perfume bottle and all the tools except the nail file are of silver gilt and marked with a boar's head for Paris after 1838. Not all of these walnuts are fitted with a silver gilt frame and silver gilt tools. Quite often a less expensive version is found that has a frame and tools of gilt metal which, consequently, commands a lower price.

Colour Plate 139. Lady's Companions. One of tortoiseshell inlaid with mother-of-pearl and another of mother-of-pearl edged with abalone shell. The green lining beautifully complements the abalone shell. Some of these sets have a post under the thimble that lifts up to reveal a small cavity that was used to hold packets of needles. English. c.1840. Height 4¼in. (10.9cm.)

Punch marks on French sewing sets are often difficult to decipher but if clear the following may be of help to collectors:-

1809 – 1819	Cock's head	–	Paris gold
1819 – 1838	Cock	–	gold and silver
	Rabbit's head	–	Paris silver
After 1838	Eagle's head	–	Paris gold
	Horse's head	–	Provinces' gold
	Boar's head	–	Paris silver
	Crab	–	Provinces' silver

Sewing sets in England at this same period fall into two categories. There were flat cases, usually of leather, that held sterling silver tools, or there were standing boxed sets known as Lady's Companions. Lady's Companions were made from

Colour Plate 140. English sterling silver sewing set in tortoiseshell case. The fittings are a tape-measure, waxer, thimble and emery cushion. c.1840.

mother-of-pearl, tortoiseshell or tooled leather and the examples illustrated (Colour Plate 139) show how the tortoiseshell was beautifully inlaid with mother-of-pearl and the mother-of-pearl edged with abalone shell. These Lady's Companions have always been thought to date from about the middle of the nineteenth century, however, the tortoiseshell example has an inscription 'C M 15th July, 1839' and another similar example has an inscription dated 1834. The interiors of these boxes are lined with satin and/or velvet and a folding needlebook is made from the same lining material. This needlebook also held skeins of silk and a pair of scissors slid into a flap on the outside. A notepad of ivory was always included and usually a mirror. A variety of other tools was included – a pencil, knife, ruler, bodkin, tape-measure and occasionally even a perfume bottle. A thimble fitted over a post and sometimes when this post is gently pulled up a cavity underneath is revealed. The mother-of-pearl example illustrated not only has a cavity but found inside this cavity were two packets of needles made by Edwd Perks and dated 1841. Of course the date of a packet of needles included in any sewing box or sewing set is not a guide to the date of that container as one has no knowledge as to when or why such items were included.

Although most English sewing sets were leather cased, occasionally an example is found that has sterling silver needlework tools in a tortoiseshell case. Colour Plate 140 shows such an example and the sterling silver tools – a tape-measure, waxer, thimble and emery cushion have matching patterns.

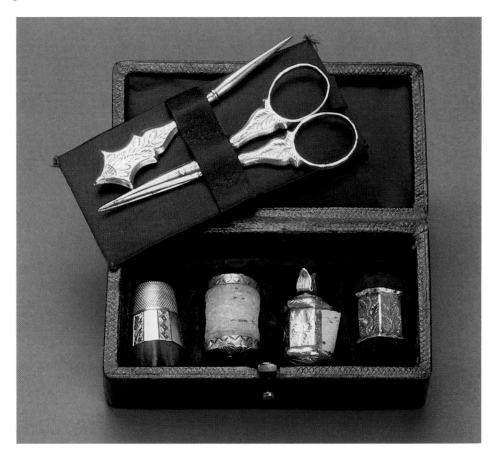

Colour Plate 141. Sewing set of sterling silver with bright cut decoration in a leather case. A thimble, waxer, tape-measure and emery cushion fit into the base of the box and the tray holding a stiletto and scissors fits on top. English. c.1840.

Colour Plate 142. Leather boxed sterling silver sewing set. These needlework tools are now known to have been made by Joseph Taylor. His mark, 'IT', is sometimes found underneath the handle of the basket pincushion or amongst the scrolling decoration on other tools. English. Early 19th century.

Another English sterling silver sewing set (Colour Plate 141) has a leather case and the four tools that fit into the base of the box are a thimble, waxer, tape-measure and emery cushion. Sometimes this variety of boxed set also has a sterling silver pencil in the base. A material covered tray fits over the four tools in the base of the box and this tray holds a stiletto and scissors with handles of bright

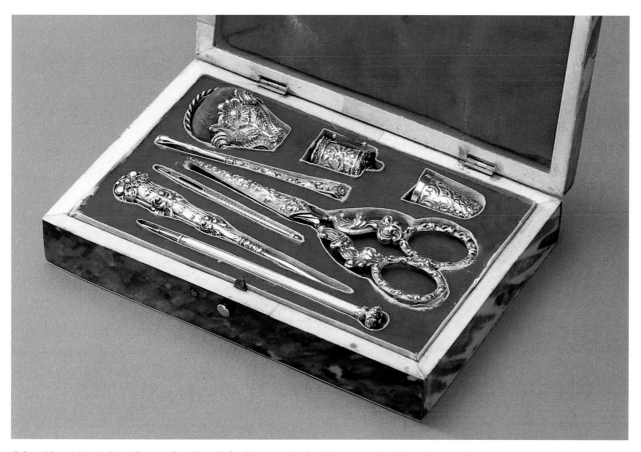

Colour Plate 143. Sterling silver needlework tools fitted into a red velvet lined tortoiseshell box. These tools, also made by Joseph Taylor, are a basket pincushion, tape-measure, thimble, combination ear-spoon/tweezers, scissors with protective sheath, bodkin, stiletto and pencil. English. Early 19th century. Box 5¾ x 4in. (14.6x 10.2cm.)

cut sterling silver that match the pattern of the other pieces. The silk tape-measures in these last two sets are original and are marked in inches.

The sewing set in Colour Plate 142 is a variety that quite frequently comes onto the market. It is the one sewing set that does not have matching pieces but care must be taken to ensure that the pieces are original. Even though the patterns on some of the pieces are different, the pieces all blend together and 'look right'. It is quite common for the shell pattern on the thimble, basket pincushion and knife to be combined with a pair of scissors with handles in a grape pattern. These leather boxed sterling silver sewing sets were made by Joseph Taylor and although never hallmarked the maker's mark 'IT' can often be found on at least one of the needlework tools. While the most likely place to find this mark is underneath the handle on the basket pincushion, it is often found on the needlecase as well. Various tools were fitted into these boxes. They always seem to have a pair of scissors, thimble, tweezers with ear-spoon, bodkin, tape-measure and stiletto but additional tools to complete these sets will be a basket pincushion, a knife or a needlecase.

The majority of sterling silver sets of needlework tools made by Joseph Taylor are fitted into leather boxes, but occasionally a more prestigious box has been made of tortoiseshell to hold a similar tray of tools to those found in a leather box. The tortoiseshell box (Colour Plate 143) holds very similar sterling silver tools to those in the leather box discussed previously. There are slight differences, however, in that the basket pincushion ·in the tortoiseshell box is more elaborate

Colour Plate 144. Miniature sewing sets in egg-shaped containers of painted tin, amber glass with gilt metal framework and floral and blue enamel. Two of these miniature sets are made of silver gilt, the other of gilt metal. French. Mid 19th century. Length 3½in. (9cm.)

Colour Plate 145. French egg-shaped containers for miniature sewing tools. The two halves of the mother-of-pearl example when closed clip shut under the brass bird finial. The blue opaline glass egg sits on a nest of gilt metal. Both miniature sewing sets are made of gilt metal and although very small are all in working order. c.1870. Height of mother-of-pearl example 5in. (12.7cm.)

although the tools in the back rows of both boxes are the same, i.e. basket pincushion, tape-measure and thimble. Both boxes have scissors with a sheath, bodkin and combination tweezers/ear-spoon but the tortoiseshell box has two additional tools - a stiletto and pencil. Joseph Taylor is acknowledged as an English silversmith of the highest calibre and this is certainly apparent when examining sets of his needlework tools.

Mid nineteenth century sewing sets in egg-shaped containers were another French frivolity. The eggs (Colour Plate 144) were made from either painted tin, enamel or glass and were carried on the finger by a ring. Two of the illustrated examples have fittings of silver gilt while the enamel egg has tools of gilt metal. The tools in these eggs are usually a thimble, scissors, stiletto, bodkin and needle-case and although small are in perfect working order.

Slightly later in the century, two other French sewing sets were produced (Colour Plate 145), again with the container an egg-shape. The two halves of the mother–of–pearl example when closed clip shut under the brass bird finial and the blue opaline glass egg sits on a gilt metal nest. The tools in these sets are far too small for easy use and one wonders if they were produced at an afternoon sewing circle purely for reasons of 'one-upmanship'.

Colour Plate 146. Brass fish that holds a miniature sewing set. This set could be worn hanging by a ribbon from the waist. c.1870. Length 4in. (10.2cm.)

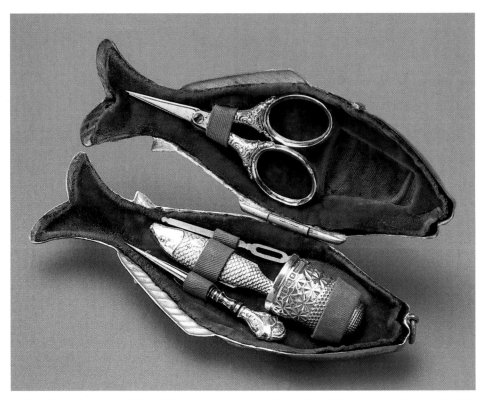

Colour Plate 147. Interior of brass fish sewing set shown in Colour Plate 146. A pair of scissors, a thimble, stiletto, bodkin and needlecase in the shape of a fish fit inside this container. c.1870.

Another miniature sewing set (Colour Plates 146 & 147) has silver tools inside a brass fish and as it has a ring at its mouth it was possibly worn hanging from the waist. Again, although small, the pieces are in good working order and could well have been used. The small silver fish needlecase is especially delightful.

A purse, to hold one's sewing tools and small pieces of embroidery, was a very useful fashion accessory during the 1870s and 1880s. *The Ladies Magazine* in July, 1872 published just one of many patterns for a diligent needlewoman to make her own 'Case for Working Implements' (Plate 9). Numerous other magazines featured different styles and, as a consequence, commercially made sewing purses

Colour Plate 148. Sewing purse of dark blue velvet trimmed with bands of ivory. Gilt metal needlework tools are fitted into one of the flaps of this purse – the needlecase is missing. French. c.1880. Width 5½in. (14cm.)

became available. The dark blue velvet and gilt metal purse shown in Colour Plate 148 has been trimmed with strips of ivory to create a most dramatic effect. This purse flaps open, one flap being fitted with a pincushion, the other with an incomplete set of gilt metal needlework tools. The rigid ends of this cylindrical purse do not open but similar purses have ends that open, one end being a money purse and the other fitted with gilt metal tools for crocheting.

Plate 9. Illustration of a 'Case for Working Implements' that was published with instructions. From The Ladies Magazine, *1872.*

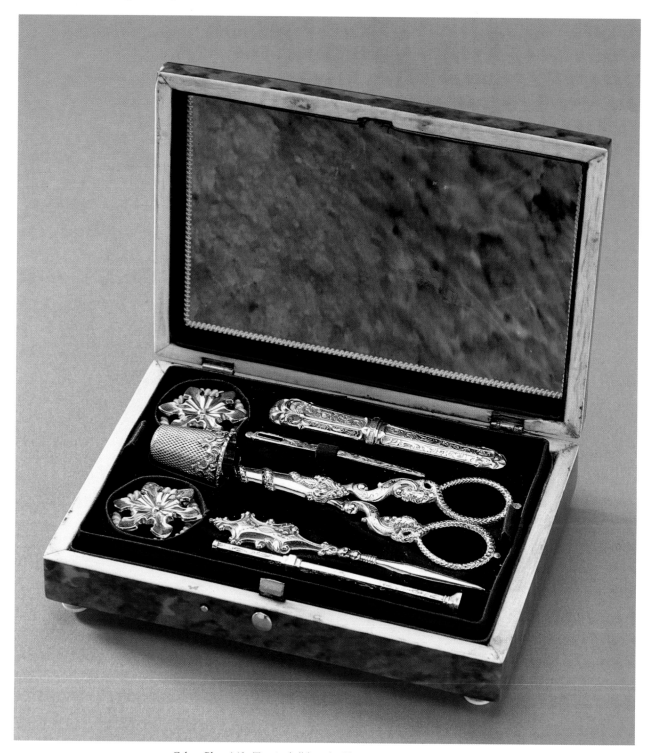

Colour Plate 149. Tortoiseshell boxed gold sewing set. Workmanship of the highest quality has produced these superb needlework tools. Dutch. Late 19th century. Box 5 x 3½in. (12.7 x 9cm.)

The gold sewing set (Colour Plate 149) fits into a blue velvet tray inside a tortoiseshell box. This tortoiseshell box is quite distinctive as the tortoiseshell in the lid is extremely thin and almost transparent. The gold tools are superbly made and have a Dutch mark. Similar sets have been viewed by the author that have been owned for generations by Dutch families. The tools contained in this box

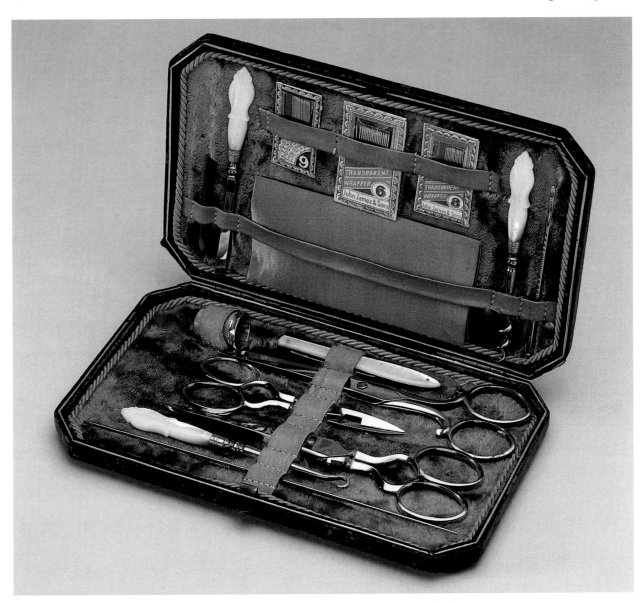

Colour Plate 150. Utilitarian late Victorian English sewing set. A vast number of similar sets in leatherette cases were produced and are just as useful today as when they were originally made. Only one knitting needle is still in place in the front of the box. Late 19th century. Box 7½ x 4¾in. (19.1 x 12.1cm.)

are a needlecase, bodkin, thimble, scissors, stiletto, pencil and two silk winders.

Towards the end of the nineteenth century sets in flat boxes were produced by both English and French manufacturers. A vast number of these utilitarian English sets are still to be found and are just as useful today as when they were originally made. The example seen in Colour Plate 150 is typical of these English sets and holds the usual complement of needlework tools – packets of needles, a fabric needlebook, bodkin, thimble and three sizes of scissors including buttonhole scissors. The additional tools are quite usual and are a pencil, tweezers, corkscrew to open small bottles of perfume, folding knife and button hook. Originally this box would have contained a set of four steel knitting needles but only one is still in place.

French silver sewing sets made towards the end of the nineteenth century have plain flat leatherette cases. In comparison, the contents are quite glorious and the

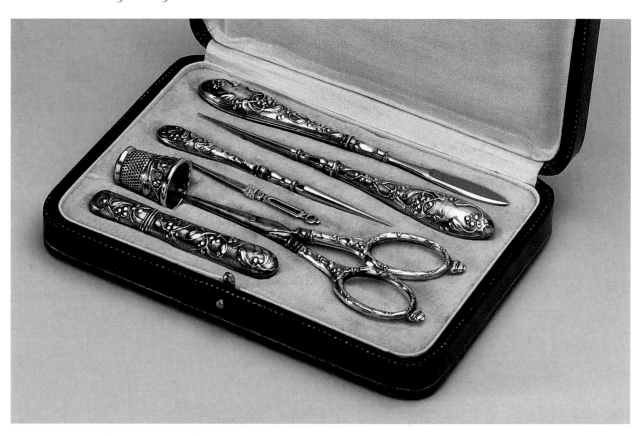

Colour Plate 151. French silver sewing set in a leatherette case. The seam cutter, crochet hook, stiletto, bodkin, scissors and needlecase are original fittings and feature the popular mistletoe design. This design has also been used to decorate the thimble but it is a replacement and is English. Late 19th century. Box 5½ x 3¾in. (14 x 9.6cm.)

Colour Plate 152. German silver sewing set in a leatherette case. The designs featured in this glorious set depict the different ages in a lady's life. Each piece is marked with a French import mark. Late 19th century. Box 7 x 5½in. (17.8 x 14cm.)

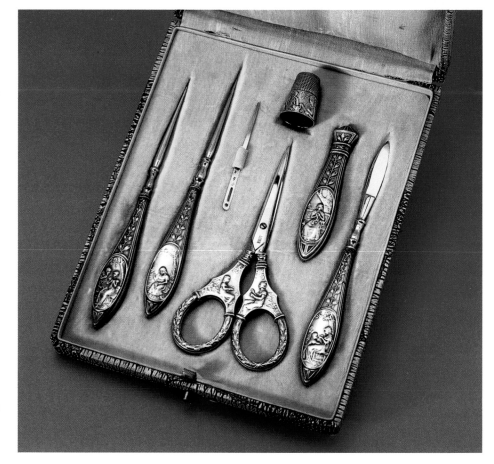

Colour Plate 153. American sterling silver egg-shaped sewing set made by Simons Bros. with original thimble, both bearing the imprint 'PAT. May 31, 98'. Length 2¼in. (5.8cm.)

mistletoe design, in repoussé, is featured in Colour Plate 151. The French silver tools in this set are a seam cutter, crochet hook, stiletto, bodkin, scissors and needlecase, however, the thimble that has a matching design is a replacement and is English. It is not unusual for a thimble from a sewing set to be mislaid after use and finding a suitable replacement is usually quite difficult.

Another silver sewing set (Colour Plate 152) was also made at the end of the nineteenth century. This set is particularly interesting as at first glance it appears to be of French origin and has a Nice, France retailer's name in the lid of the box. However, each piece of this set has three clear marks and a study of *International Hallmarks on Silver* by Tardy makes it possible to interpret them. The first mark is 800 which denotes the fineness of the silver. The second mark is a crown and moon which was placed on German silver after 1st January, 1888. The third mark is a French import mark that was put on silver of a standard of fineness of at least 800 from 1st July 1864 to 30th June, 1893. This set must have been made, therefore, in Germany and imported into France between 1st January, 1888 and 30th June, 1893. This set, in pristine condition, features a lady sewing – each needlework tool depicting a different stage of her life and beginning with her as a young girl, as shown on the stiletto. The tools included in this set are identical to the tools with the mistletoe design.

American silver manufacturing companies produced an abundance of sterling silver needlework tools at the end of the nineteenth century. It is not surprising therefore, that at least one company made a decorative sterling silver egg that held packets of needles, pins and a thimble (Colour Plate 153). This sewing set was made by Simons Bros. Co., the prestigious American silversmiths and the egg as well as the thimble have their maker's mark and imprint of 'PAT. MAY 31, 98'. The three packets of needles that date from the 1890s fit into unusual curved slots.

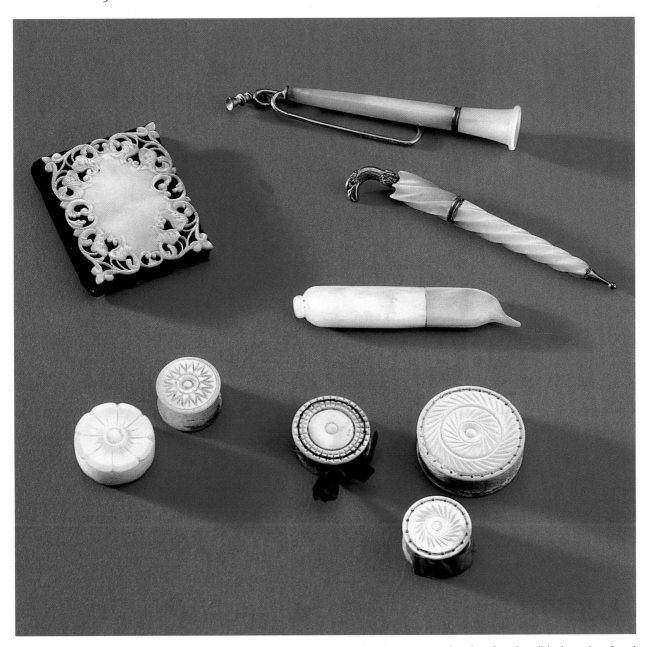

Colour Plate 155. Mother-of-pearl needlework tools. Rear:- carved mother-of-pearl needlebook, mother-of-pearl needlecases in the shape of a trumpet, umbrella and peapod. Front:- flat disc varieties of waxers (two sizes), two emery cushions and a pincushion. Early Victorian. Length of trumpet needlecase 4in. (10.2cm.)

Chapter Nine
Victorian Sewing Tools

The early Victorian era was the era of mother-of-pearl. Sewing boxes were filled with reel holders, emery cushions, pincushions, needlecases, waxers and tape-measures – all decorated with beautifully carved mother-of-pearl. The variety of glorious patterns of mother-of-pearl reel holders can be seen in Colour Plate 154, even extending to some reels having small mirrors in the centre of the mother-of-pearl. Some of these reel holders have ivory posts that unscrew, others have a brass post attached to the base of the reel that slots into the brass post attached to the decorative top of the reel. The bases are usually made from bone but some of the more ornate reel holders have bases of mother-of-pearl.

The emery cushions, waxers and tape-measures that fit into slots in Victorian sewing boxes have only the tops carved from mother-of-pearl, because this is the only section visible when the pieces are in position in the tray of the box. A set of waxer, emery cushion, and tape-measure with matching carved mother-of-pearl tops can be seen in the centre of Colour Plate 154 while Colour Plate 113 shows

Colour Plate 154. Needlework tools with mother-of-pearl tops that were the fittings found in Victorian sewing boxes as shown in Colour Plate 113. On the left are varieties of reels (in pairs) showing the beauty that was achieved with carved mother-of-pearl. The centre pair have tiny mirrors fitted into the tops. On the right of this photo are a set of six matching reels with carved mother-of-pearl tops. Centre:- a waxer, emery and tape-measure also with matching mother-of-pearl tops. These are the three tools that fit into recesses in the front of Victorian sewing boxes (see Colour Plate 113). Early to mid Victorian. Height of tallest reel 1¾in. (4.5cm.)

a Victorian sewing box with these three needlework tools fitted into their respective slots at the front of the box. The cylindrical frame of the emery cushion and tape-measure is made from bone. It is important that the fabric holding the emery inside the frame is still intact and that the tape-measure still has its original silk tape which is usually marked in inches. The bases of these waxers are made from bone and some collectors prefer to own a waxer that has wax worn into ridges, where thread has been pulled along it. It is interesting to note how often needlewomen today, especially quilters, still wax their thread even though commercially waxed thread is readily available.

When a Victorian lady purchased her sewing box she was able to choose which carved mother-of-pearl design she preferred on the top of the fitted needlework tools. It was usual for a matching pattern to be used on the reels, emery cushion, waxer and tape-measure. However, collectors today often find it impossible to buy a matching set of mother-of-pearl fittings and consequently fit a sewing box with pieces that have a variety of carved mother-of-pearl tops. This variety can be more appealing to a collector than a matching set.

Waxers, emery cushions and pincushions were also made in flat disc shapes (Colour Plate 155), the wax or cushion fitting between two discs of carved mother-of-pearl. Emery cushions are usually smaller in size than pincushions and the emery content can be determined by either weight (emery makes the cushion considerably heavier) or by gently pushing a fine needle into the cushion to feel the grains of emery.

More ornate mother-of-pearl pincushions, needlecases and needlebooks were made both in England and France, none quite reaching the perfection of the earlier mother-of-pearl tools sold at the Palais Royal. The selection also shown in Colour Plate 155 is extremely interesting and shows the tremendous ingenuity of the craftsmen. The mother-of-pearl pod needlecase is a slightly different shape to the ivory peapod needlecases carved in Dieppe (Colour Plate 85) and mother-of-pearl has been used with a gilt frame to create unusual needlecases in the form of an umbrella and a trumpet. Mother-of-pearl was frequently used, either fretted or carved, for the covers of needlebooks and the illustrated example is quite delightful.

Victorian needlework tools were fashioned from every possible material and the examples in Colour Plate 156 are made of glass or porcelain. The glass cylindrical needlecase is especially fragile as it has only a cardboard frame to support the thin glass. The glass on the three disc pincushions has been used to protect the hand painted prints underneath and sometimes a mirror is attached to the other side. The pincushion on the left is extremely interesting as it portrays the popular comedy character Paul Pry and is inscribed along the top with his catch phrase 'I hope I don't intrude'. The glass pincushion in the centre is a memorial to the poet William Wordsworth and shows his tombstone (died 1850) shared with his wife Mary (died 1859). The predominant tombstone is that of Wordsworth's

Colour Plate 156. Rear:- three pincushions with paintings under glass. Front:- glass needlecase and two porcelain reels. Early Victorian. Length of needlecase 3½in. (9cm.)

beloved daughter Dora (1817 – 1847). The third glass pincushion is a commemorative of the Crystal Palace – that magnificent building constructed in Hyde Park, London, to house The Great Exhibition of All Nations in 1851. Other needlework tools were produced to commemorate this historic event and are keenly sought by collectors.

The porcelain reels for thread have been delightfully painted and are quite rare. They were usually found as fittings in Continental sewing boxes often with matching porcelain perfume bottles.

Straw-work, paper and horn have been used for the needlework tools in Colour

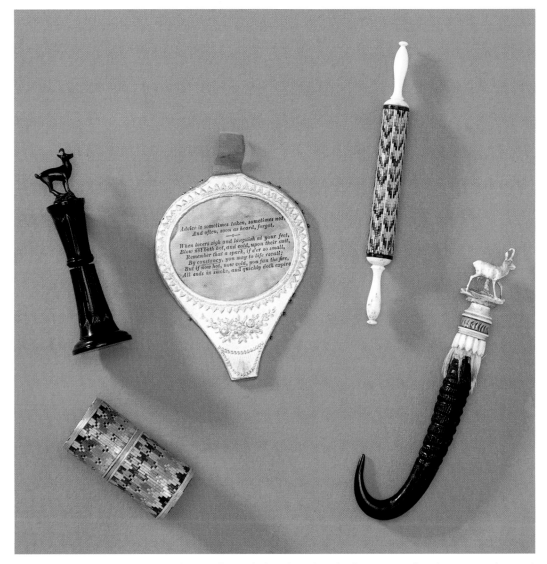

Colour Plate 157. Two horn needlecases, both with antelope finials. Centre:- silk and paper pincushion with typical Victorian poignant verses. Also shown – a needlecase in the shape of a rolling pin made of bone and straw-work and a straw-work cylinder that holds wax. Early Victorian. Length of rolling pin needlecase 4in. (10.2cm.)

Plate 157. The art of using coloured straw for a decorative effect, previously discussed in Chapter 3, continued into the Victorian era and the larger cylinder, front left, of this colour plate holds a piece of wax. The needlecase on the right has been made to resemble a rolling pin and one of the bone handles unscrews so that needles can be stored in the hollow cylinder. The central pincushion has been made from paper that has been embossed and painted with a gold highlight. The back has been covered with pink silk and the pins are inserted around the circumference. The oval section has been printed with two verses the first reading:-

> Advice is sometimes taken, sometimes not,
> And often, soon as heard, forgot.

Victorians loved to use homilies! The second poignant verse reads:-

> When <u>lovers </u> sigh and languish at your feet,
> Blow not both <u>hot</u>, and <u>cold</u>, upon their suit,

Colour Plate 158. Needlework tools fashioned from wood. Rear:- standing figural needlecases – Tyrolean. Front:- two painted wooden holders for packets of needles and a painted winder – Scandinavian. Also shown a rare wooden needlecase in the shape of a peapod. Early Victorian. Length of peapod needlecase 4in. (10.2cm.)

> Remember that a spark, if e'er so small,
> By <u>constancy</u>, you may to life recall;
> But if now <u>hot</u>, now <u>cold</u>, you fan the fire,
> All ends in smoke, and quickly doth expire.

Some previous owner has underlined some of the words in this verse in pencil. One wonders why?

The two remaining needlecases in this colour plate are made from horn. The one with a carved horn antelope as a finial pulls open at the centre, the other, with a bone antelope finial, has been made from a small but complete antelope's horn and this needlecase opens by unscrewing the finial.

Craftsmen have always fashioned small containers from a variety of woods. The group in Colour Plate 158 are typical of those produced in different countries. The tall needlecases with a man and a lady standing on a pedestal (that pulls open to hold needles) are typical of Tyrolean souvenirs made during the third quarter of

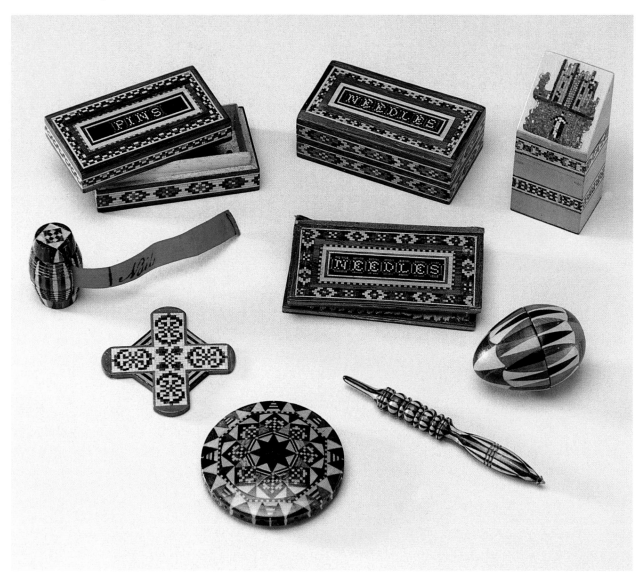

Colour Plate 159. Tunbridge ware needlework tools. Rear:- boxes for pins and needles and a standing needlebox for packets of needles in graduating sizes. Centre:- tape-measure, needlebook and egg-shaped thimble holder. Front:- winder, disc-shaped pincushion and lace pricker. c.1840. Length of lace pricker 3¼in. (8.3cm.)

the nineteenth century. The two painted wooden boxes have both been utilised for packets of needles and they and the painted wooden silk winder are of Scandinavian origin, probably Denmark. The wooden peapod needlecase is identical to the ivory examples made in the Dieppe region of France (Colour Plate 85). It is ironical that wooden peapod needlecases are quite rare whereas examples carved from ivory are not difficult to find.

The exacting craft of Tunbridge ware was not only used to decorate sewing boxes, pleat boxes and boxes to hold reels for thread (Colour Plate 119). It was also used on numerous small needlework requisites (Colour Plate 159) and could be utilised so that not only geometric and Berlin woolwork patterns were produced, but wood mosaic letters formed the word describing the contents. Examples of boxes for pins and needles are illustrated as well as a needlebook that has flannel pages to hold the needles. The needlebox at the back on the right of this colour plate held packets of needles of graduating sizes standing upright. The

Colour Plate 160. Tunbridge ware reel holder. The pattern on the base of this example closely resembles one of the patterns seen in the Berlin woolwork sampler (Colour Plate 121). c.1840. Length 5in. (12.7cm.)

mosaic inlay on the sloped lid of the box depicts an Abbess standing outside an Abbey. The egg-shaped container unscrews at the centre and holds a brass thimble and the barrel-shaped container holds a silk tape-measure marked in nails. The disc pincushion has a different pattern on each side and pins fit into holes in the wood around the circumference. The silk winder has an identical pattern on each side because it has been sliced from a solid piece of wood mosaic. The last needlework tool in this colour plate is a rare Tunbridge ware lace pricker. In this instance the steel pricker is permanently attached to the Tunbridge ware handle and a cover screws over the steel pricker to protect it when not in use. The lace pricker in this colour plate is shown with the cover in place. Sometimes these lace prickers are found with the covers missing as they are often mislaid when the pricker is in constant use.

An interesting Tunbridge ware reel holder is shown in Colour Plate 160 and a delightful mosaic vignette of a rabbit decorates the centre of the base of this stand. By pulling the knob on the side of the right-hand post, the steel rod supporting the reel of thread can be removed, facilitating reel replacement. Another delightful feature are the four bun feet – two being visible in the colour plate.

Until George Baxter invented the process of colour printing all black and white printing had to be coloured by hand. Baxter, after working in his father's printing and publishing business started on his own in 1829 and during the next five years experimented with processes of printing in colour. The brilliant research undertaken by C.T. Courtney Lewis gives us the chronological order of the vast number of colour prints Baxter produced and a pattern emerges of how his

Colour Plate 161. Baxter prints 'Queen's Floral Needle-box Set'. The ten small floral pictures were used to decorate the top of small boxes that held packets of needles. The large floral picture decorated the lid of the box that held these ten small boxes. 1850. Size of set of ten prints 6 x 4in. (15.2 x 10.2cm.)

interest progressed from book illustrations to the needle-box prints that are of great interest to collectors of needlework tools.

By the 1840s sewing needles were being produced in great quantities. The average person could now afford to buy a packet of needles whereas previously it was only possible to own an individual needle. Little cardboard boxes were made to hold these packets of needles. These boxes measured approximately one inch (2.6 cm.) by nearly two inches (5.2 cm.) and were nearly half an inch (1.3 cm.) deep. Baxter printed pictures to decorate the top of these boxes and thus the idea of needle-box prints was born.

The first set produced in 1850 was called 'The Regal Set'. Ten little pictures were printed on one sheet 12½ x 2¼in. (32 x 5.8 cm.). This set, as the name implies, centres around the Royal family. As well as pictures of Queen Victoria and Prince Albert, Royal residencies and occasions are featured.

The next set to be produced was the 'Queen's Floral Needle-box Set' (Colour Plate 161). The first sheet in this series is of 10 small 'bouquets' of flowers and was produced usually with a blue background, although green or buff are to be found. As well as a sheet of 10 little pictures to be used on the small cardboard boxes, larger prints were produced of a bouquet of flowers to decorate the top of a large box. Sometimes the ten cardboard boxes of needles were packed into a 6 x 4in. (15.2 x 10.2cm.) cardboard box and Baxter decorated the top of this box with the large bouquet print. In case a box was needed to hold only 3 or 6 tiny needle-boxes, prints were made in various sizes for this purpose. This set is marked 'Baxter' on each picture.

Another ten picture sheet named 'Tarantella Set' was produced in a similar manner in 1850. This set has an assortment of pictures and is signed.

Towards the end of 1850 two sets of needle-box prints were produced with a difference. These are 'The Greek Dance' and 'The Harem Set'. Here, two strips of pictures 5 x 1¾in. (12.7 x 4.5 cm.) were made and at first glance the whole

Colour Plate 162. Baxter print 'The Allied Sovereigns and the Commanders of their Forces'. These ten pictures were used to decorate the top of ten small boxes that held packets of needles. 1855. 5½ x 4in. (14 x 10.2cm.)

strip appears to be one picture. However, a closer look at this picture reveals it is actually five individual pictures joined together to make a delightful scene.

It is two years before Baxter produced another set, this again being two strips aptly named 'Religious Events'. It is thought that this set as well as being used for needle-boxes was used for Sunday School cards.

In 1855 Baxter produced two strips of needle-box prints, 'Fairy Scenes' and 'Pas des Trois'. Again a lovely picture can be divided up into individual scenes. In this same year a patriotic theme abounded with a set called 'The Allied Sovereigns and the Commanders of their Forces' (Colour Plate 162). In this set ten portraits are depicted of personalities associated with the Crimean War. Initially produced with a portrait of Marshall St. Arnaud, when he died this was replaced by a portrait of Empress Eugénie and this latter set is the rarer and more valuable.

'The Queen and the Heroes of India' was produced in 1857 and this is another set of ten oval portraits. It was published at the time of the Indian Mutiny.

The years 1858 and 1859 saw the production of the last two sets of needle-box prints. 'The May Queen Set' included portraits of The Princess Royal and Prince Frederick of Prussia and coincided with their marriage. 'Figures and Landscapes Set' is another set of oval prints but in this set each print is set off by a scroll mount.

Numerous printers began using Baxter's process of colouring printing under licence but the only printing firm with ability equal to Baxter was Le Blond & Co.

Colour Plate 163. Le Blond print 'The Regal Set'. These ten pictures were printed as a sheet, then cut and used individually to decorate the lids of small boxes that held packets of needles. About 1850. 5 x 3½in. (12.7 x 9cm.)

Colour Plate 164. Le Blond print 'The Fancy Subject Set'. This print usually accompanies Colour Print 163 'The Regal Set'. They are the only two prints produced by Le Blond to decorate boxes for packets of needles. About 1850. 5 x 3½in. (12.7 x 9cm.)

About 1850 this firm produced two sets of needle-box prints and these were called 'The Regal Set' and 'The Fancy Subject Set' (Colour Plates 163 & 164). Le Blond's Regal Set must not be confused with the set of the same name produced by Baxter. Each set has ten individual pictures and Courtney Lewis names and fully describes each print in these Le Blond sets in the same manner he individually describes each of the Baxter sets.

The quality of needle-box prints is all important. Up to twelve wood blocks were used for different colours during the printing process and there is often a marked difference in the vibrancy of colours in different copies of the same set. Sometimes it is thought that one or two blocks were omitted during the colour printing process which is, of course, possible. However, the variation in colour appears more often to be due to exposure to bright light.

Three needle-boxes are shown in Colour Plate 165, the two on the left have been fitted with ormolu mounts. The box first on the left has the print 'The May Queen' from the set of that same name (Reference C.L. No. 144 date 1858). The print on the second needle-box is from the Religious Events Set No. 2 (Ref. C.L. No. 139 date 1852) and is called 'Christ Blessing Bread'. The third needle-box is decorated with a Le Blond print and it is from Le Blond's 'Fancy Subject Set' and is named 'The Flower Maiden' (Ref. C.L. No. 73 date about 1850). The round pincushion has also been fitted with an ormolu mount over a print of Queen

Colour Plate 165. Top:- three small boxes with lids decorated with needle-box prints (details see text). Bottom:- round pincushion with ormolu mount featuring Baxter's print of Queen Victoria; needlebook decorated with Baxter's print of His Royal Highness the Prince of Wales. 1850 to 1855. Diameter of pincushion 2in. (5.2cm.)

Victoria from the Baxter set 'The Allied Sovereigns and the Commanders of their Forces' (Ref. C.L. No. 142 date 1855). The needlebook on the right of this colour plate has been made from strong cardboard and has sections inside to hold packets of needles. One of Baxter's prints 'His Royal Highness Prince of Wales' (Ref. C.L. No. 211 date 1850) has been used for the front cover and the print 'Windsor Castle' (Ref. C.L. No. 281 date 1850) has been used on the back cover.

George Baxter was a brilliant inventor but an unsuccessful businessman and after endless problems was declared bankrupt in 1865. He died in January 1867 after being hit by a horse-drawn omnibus the previous year. A sad end to this brilliant inventor who contributed so much to the advancement of the colour printing process.

Colour Plate 166. A rare complete set of needle-boxes decorated with needle-box prints. This set of prints, 'The New Ten', was published by Vincent Brooks in 1866. This colour plate illustrates how each small print was cut from the sheet of ten prints and used to decorate each of the lids in this boxed set. 5¼ x 4in. (14.6 x 10.2cm.)

Private Collector.

Vincent Brooks, listed as a Lithographer, purchased some of Baxter's colour blocks in 1865 or 1866 possibly through the negotiations of Baxter's son who was now his employee. Brooks did re-publish some of Baxter's prints and included at that time a set of needle-box prints of his own devising. This set was called 'The New Ten' and a boxed set of these needle-boxes decorated with these rare prints is shown in Colour Plate 166. There is one feature about this set of needle-box prints that is not seen on any other set – each portrait is printed with the name of the subject. The sale of Vincent Brooks re-publications, which included The New Ten set of needle-box prints, was most likely held in June 1866 and as this was not a very successful venture and very few prints were sold, this complete surviving set is very rare.

The best known clamp from the Victorian era is the Hemmingbird clamp and the version sought after by collectors was made by Charles Waterman in America. This clamp, on the left of Colour Plate 167, is made from gilded brass and was used as a 'third hand' to help a needlewoman when hemming. It had two cushions, one on the bird's back and one beneath the bird, on the clamp. If the metal is not too worn around the edges of the wings, one can see the words 'Patented Feb 15 1853' impressed into the metal. When used the bird is clamped firmly onto the edge of a table and by depressing the tail, the beak opens and fabric can be held firmly in the beak once the tail is released. This greatly aids the speed when hemming, especially if using waxed thread. The beak could damage

Colour Plate 167. Hemmingbird clamps. Left:- this variety was made by Charles Waterman. The edge of the wings are marked 'Patented Feb 15, 1853'. Right:- a needlecase is fitted at the front of this clamp with an acorn finial that unscrews. c.1850. Height of left clamp 5¼in. (13.4cm.)

Colour Plate 168. Cast iron clamps in the form of dolphins. Both open to hold fabric when hemming. The tail of the left example holds a pincushion. German. c.1840. Height of left clamp 9in. (22.8cm.)

*Colour Plate 169. Winding clamps used in pairs to hold skeins of silk or wool. Left pair:- wood and steel –
Italian. Right pair:- rosewood – English. Height of left example 9in. (22.8cm.)*

very fine fabric and the alternate method was to attach the end of the fabric with
a pin to the lower cushion. Numerous designs for 'bird' clamps were patented and
another variety on the right of Colour Plate 167 has a smaller bird with a
pincushion above, at the top of a post. The post at the front edge of the clamp has
an acorn finial that unscrews and reveals a hollow cylinder to be used for needles.

Man's ingenuity knew no bounds when producing varieties of hemming clamps
and instead of a bird, a butterfly, fish or frog are just some of the motifs used.
Cast-iron clamps made in Germany had a dolphin as a feature (Colour Plate 168)
and the dolphin on a shell is an example of the high standard of German
craftsmanship when working with cast-iron.

The introduction and acceptance of the sewing machine caused the demise of the
hemming clamp. Needlewomen were now released from the tedious task of hemming
long seams by hand. It is no wonder, that in a very short length of time, any woman
who could afford a sewing machine was utilising this time saving invention.

Pairs of clamps for winding thread from skeins were produced in all countries,
the wood and steel pair (Colour Plate 169) are of Italian origin and the rosewood
pair in the same colour plate are typically English. Winding clamps were attached
to the edge of a table and the distance between the clamps allowed a skein of
thread to be held firmly around the outside of the cage of both clamps. Both
hands were then free to wind the thread either into a ball or onto a winder.

Colour Plate 170. Set of three steel clamps – two winding clamps and a pincushion clamp. Facets of steel have been used to decorate the holding plate on these clamps. c.1840. Height of left clamp 9in. (22.8cm.)

Colour Plate 171. Winding clamp or swift that opens in a similar manner to an umbrella. A bone ring and screw on the central post holds the swift open. Early Victorian. Height 25½in. (64.7cm.)

Colour Plate 172. Hand coloured steel engraving showing a swift in operation. The other ladies are making lace which is discussed in Chapter 10. Mid 19th century.

Winding clamps were produced in various sizes to accommodate either small skeins of silk or large skeins of home-spun wool.

The pair of steel winding clamps in Colour Plate 170 have a matching pincushion clamp and, although not as early as the set that forms part of the fittings in the Palais Royal box in Colour Plate 46, they fulfil exactly the same purpose. The winding clamps are suitable for a variety of threads and the pincushion would be most convenient clamped onto a table near a needlewoman.

A different variety of winding clamp or swift (Colour Plate 171) looks very much like an umbrella frame. This structure of wood, clamps onto a table and the frame can be opened in exactly the same manner as opening an umbrella. The frame can be opened to fit different sized skeins of thread and held in place by tightening the screw on a bone ring, that slides up and down the central post under the frame. Sometimes other varieties of this type of swift have a weighted base and they stand on top of the table instead of being clamped to the edge. Frequently circular screw marks are seen underneath the edge of Victorian tables and these have been made by various needlework clamps. An interesting hand-coloured engraving (Colour Plate 172) shows one of these swifts in operation, in this case the base is heavy and weighted. Also shown in this print are Bruges lace makers and lace bobbins will be discussed in Chapter 10.

Steel scissors that are suitable for embroidery have been made for centuries, and scissors with folding handles were a tool usually found in eighteenth century etuis (Colour Plate 20). Steel scissors from the nineteenth century with folding handles are rarely found, however, and the mechanism that folds the handles of the scissors in the set (Colour Plate 173) is entirely different to the mechanism used on the eighteenth century scissors. These later steel scissors have handles with four hinges allowing them to fold vertically in line with the blades. The three pairs of scissors, in graduating sizes, fit neatly into sections in a leather case.

The town of Mauchline (pronounced mock-lin) lies 11¼ miles (18 km.) inland from Ayr which is on the west coast of Scotland. Mauchline is well known for its association with Robert Burns and Burns House Museum is a well known tourist attraction. This Museum houses an enormous quantity of Robert Burns memorabilia but equally important is the collection displayed of small wooden souvenirs produced in Mauchline and surrounding areas. The greater proportion of this collection are examples made by the firm of W. and A. Smith.

During the early part of the nineteenth century, manufacturers in the Mauchline area concentrated on the production of wooden snuff boxes but as the habit of snuff taking declined only those businesses that diversified were able to survive. One such firm was Smiths' Box Works who firstly went into the production of tea caddies, as tea, like snuff, benefited from being kept in an airtight container. By the middle of the nineteenth century the range of small wooden items produced was endless with the *Art-Journal* (1849) quoting Andrew Smith who said that the products of his firm 'now consist of every article which you can almost conceive it possible to make, from postage stamp boxes up to tea trays.'

The wood mostly used in the Mauchline area for small items was sycamore as this tree grows well in the British Isles. When cut, sycamore is a creamy-white colour with a close texture which darkens when exposed to the air. After varnishing, however, it attains a mellow yellowish colour.

The small wooden objects that have become known collectively as 'Mauchline Ware' are made from sycamore wood and have had a black and white transfer applied to the exterior surface that has been varnished to lessen damage. Not only were these wooden objects made in the Mauchline area but the transfers were also applied at the time of their manufacture. The precise date that a transfer was first applied to a small wooden item is not known, but it is known that during the 1850s these souvenir wares were available in great quantities.

Transfers were made to simulate pen and ink drawings. Originally they were made from engraved copper plates later changing to steel plates. The plates were made by various engravers in London, Sheffield and Birmingham. However, the transfers made from these plates were actually made by woodware manufacturers, the majority by the firm of Smiths'. The Japanese paper transfers were inked and placed ink side down onto the object being decorated. After one to two hours to allow for drying the transfer was sponged and the Japanese paper could be rubbed off with a damp cloth leaving the inked picture and writing intact.

The names of the manufacturers of Mauchline ware, apart from the well known family associated with Smiths' Box Works, are difficult to trace. Very few pieces carry the label of the manufacturer and where a label exists it is usually found to be a bookseller, fancy goods or stationery store, or a retailer of souvenir ware.

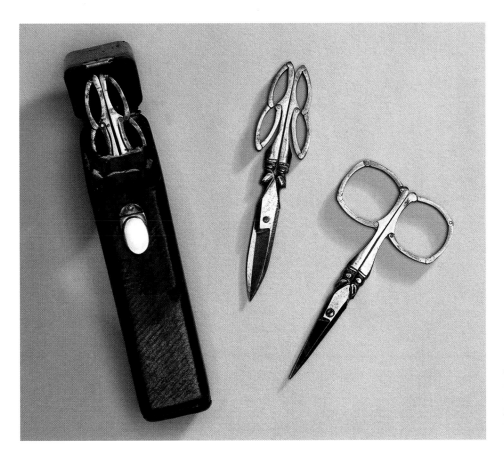

Colour Plate 173. Boxed set of steel scissors with unusual folding handles. Scissors are shown with hinged handles in different positions. Mid 19th century. Length of case when closed 5¼in. (13.4cm.)

However, a tea caddy and a cigar box are known to exist carrying the name of Davidson, Wilson & Amplhet and included in the Pinto Collection is a snuff box made by W. Johnston of Auchinleck (a village very close to Mauchline).

Enormous changes took place in England during the second half of the nineteenth century. The advent of the railways meant that for the first time people could now easily travel a distance from their village. A trip to a city or a seaside resort was of momentous importance. It is therefore quite understandable that souvenirs were extremely popular. And what a successful souvenir Mauchline Ware became, for here was a useful object with a picture to serve as a reminder of possibly a once in a lifetime event.

The variety of transfers to be found on Mauchline Ware is endless. It may be a scene, a monument, a building or a garden. The whole of the United Kingdom was covered by travellers selling these wares to retail outlets. An interesting traveller's album of sample transfers has survived that covers the south and west of England, Wales, the Midlands and north-west England. Probably another traveller covered the east and north-east of England as well as Scotland.

The popularity of Mauchline Ware spread to Europe and scenes of Cannes, Nice and Paris abound. America, India and Australia were added to the areas trading in these delightful souvenir wares and tourist resorts like Niagara Falls are the most likely American examples to be found.

As the nineteenth century progressed a large number of manufacturers purchased Mauchline Ware containers for their products. Such well known firms as Coates and Clarks had specially designed boxes made to hold their threads. A former employee of Smith's, Alexander Brown, founded the Caledonian Box Works at Lanark and established an enormous business purely as the supplier of

Colour Plate 174. Mauchline sewing box and contents. All the transfers on the box and needlework tools relate to Dunkeld and the Athole Plantations. A vast range of Mauchline tools for embroidery was made, as can be seen in this selection. Mid Victorian. Box 7½ x 4¼in (19.1 x 10.9cm.)

decorative boxes to J. and P. Coates. Alexander Brown was a keen photographer and it is thought that he was the first to use a black and white photograph instead of a transfer. It is not difficult to see the difference between an applied photograph and a transfer on Mauchline Ware. Photographs usually have a yellow or black border whereas the transfers have no distinct border.

An interesting collection of Mauchline Ware is shown in Colour Plate 174. All these needlework tools fit into the sewing box at the rear of the photo. The transfers on this box are of 'Dunkeld' and an inscription on the front of the box is as follows:-

FROM THE ATHOLE PLANTATIONS, DUNKELD.
Should auld acquaintance be forgot,
And never brought to min':
Should auld acquaintance be forgot'
And the days o' lang syne?
A. McLean & Sons Bazaar, Dunkeld

Colour Plate 175. Tartan ware needlework tools. From rear clockwise:- crochet set, needlebox, barrel-shaped container for a brass thimble, winder, shuttle and pincushion. Early Victorian. Height of thimble barrel 1¾in. (4.5cm.)

The bucket pincushion, emery cushion, tape-measure and cotton box each have a transfer of 'Dunkeld Cathedral' and the cotton box has a Highland verse on the front. The transfer on the thimble box is of 'Dunkeld House' and the needle-book 'Taymouth Castle & Loch Tay'. The transfers on the waxer and tatting shuttle are not named. Each individual piece is either inscribed 'Made of Dunkeld Wood' or 'From the Athole Plantations, Dunkeld'. A hand-written list of the contents of the box has the heading 'Contents of Granny's Work box - Marion Helen Jackson (nee Briggs) given her by her brothers when a child'. Dunkeld is a tiny Cathedral town in the wooded valley of the Tay and as each individual piece is marked A. McLean & Son this appears to be the retailer. The Athole Plantations, a source of sycamore, were located near to Dunkeld.

Another extremely popular Scottish souvenir ware is called Tartan Ware and although originally tartans were painted directly onto the wood this quickly changed to tartan patterned paper being glued to wooden objects. This process was done with such perfection it is almost impossible to see a join on some examples. The problem of joins on curved surfaces was solved by painting a black line on the wooden object where the join would occur then if there was a gap it would be less obvious. Numerous tartans were used to decorate small wooden objects and some manufacturers, certainly Smith, printed or transferred in gold lettering the name of the clan tartan onto the souvenir.

The examples illustrated (Colour Plate 175) are a needlebox (McBeth tartan), a crochet set (Frazer tartan), thimble holder in the shape of a barrel with a brass thimble (Prince Charles tartan), a pincushion (Prince Charlie tartan), a tatting shuttle (McLean tartan) and a winder (Albert tartan).

Fern Ware was another variation of Scottish souvenir ware. It now appears to have been introduced in the 1870s but it never became as popular as Mauchline or Tartan ware. Actual ferns from the Isle of Arran were originally used as a stencil. The ferns were attached to the wooden background, the whole item spattered with a pigment and when dry and the fern was removed the fern outline was highlighted by hand. Seaweed was also used in this manner, but this time-consuming method of decorating was replaced by fern patterned paper that was applied in the same way as tartan paper.

Needlework tools that have been fitted with a stanhope view are another fascinating souvenir collectable. Known also as 'peeps' these items are fitted with a miniature lens that magnifies pictures. It may be a drawing, a print or a photograph - all is revealed when one looks through the peep hole.

The tiny glass rod lens was the invention of Lord Charles Stanhope who lived between 1753 - 1816. Of course this was only one of Lord Stanhope's inventions and in his day he was better known as a flamboyant English politician. The life of Lord Stanhope is fascinating to research as his political bills introduced into Parliament were extremely progressive and his inventions were as diverse as a calculating machine and a steam vessel.

Stanhope invented a microscopic glass lens that was shaped like a glass rod about one-tenth of an inch (0.26 cm.) in diameter and one quarter inch (0.65 cm.) in length. One end of the rod is highly convex which produces a high magnification at a very short focal length. The other end of the rod is flat and has a tiny image in its centre no more than one-thirtieth of an inch in diameter – in fact the image can fit on the head of a pin.

Between 1826 and 1839 J.N. Niepce and L.J.M. Daguerre in France and W.H. Fox-Talbot in England made advances in methods of photography. These researches were studied and improved upon by John Benjamin Dancer, an English instrument maker. Dancer attached a microscope lens to a daguerreotype camera and made the world's first microphotograph. After Daguerre's death Dancer worked on the invention of the first collodion microfilm to use in his own microfilm camera. He mounted the images onto microscope slides and gave them to his friends. Interest was so great that Dancer supplied slides to novelty dealers in Manchester, in fact, they became a major part of his business.

In 1856, Dancer gave his friend Sir David Brewster several samples of his microphotographs. To view these Brewster used his invention of a thick lens, known as the 'Coddington magnifier'. During 1856 and 1857 Brewster travelled exhibiting Dancer's microphotographs and his magnifier and it was during this trip that René Dagron saw the exhibition in Paris.

There is no doubt that René Dagron was the one to see the possibilities of Dancer's invention. He was commercially orientated and could see the financial benefits. Dagron conceived the idea of affixing a micro-image onto the miniature lens. He was well aware of the demand for novelty items and this was where he directed his attention.

Dagron was granted the first microfilm patent in France (No. 23115) on 21st June, 1859. This was for 'a novelty microscope giving an illusion of depth'. He introduced his 'microscope – bijous' and such was his success that he was soon employing 150 men. Dagron was certainly a shrewd businessman. He took out a British patent in 1860 (28th March) and a U.S. Patent on 13th August that same year. Dagron continued to improve and adapt his invention and in 1861 took out another British patent No. 2347. However, regardless of all the patents Dagron held, he lost a case brought against him by a group of Parisian opticians. Dagron in his evidence maintained that he did not claim to be the inventor of the microphotograph or the lens, but he was the originator of the idea of incorporating the two in trinkets. From that date the field was open to mass manufacture and an endless variety of items were produced as can be evidenced in Douglas Jull's book on stanhopes.

In 1862 Dagron exhibited at The World's Fair in London and presented a set of microphotographs to Queen Victoria. He received an Honourable Mention in 1867 at the Exposition Universelle. One of the highlights of Dagron's career was in 1870. Emperor Napoleon III had declared war on Prussia (19th July) and by September, Paris was surrounded by Prussians. Dagron left Paris by hot-air balloon and established a system of sending news on microfilm, that was incorporated in a stanhope lens, in and out of Paris by carrier pigeon.

Dagron continued to manufacture, exhibited at the 1878 Exposition in Paris and again at The World's Fair in 1889. He died, aged 81 on the 13th June, 1900.

The variety of objects containing stanhopes is endless and once again they made wonderful souvenirs especially as the views depicted popular towns, resorts, spas etc. The views were not only of places in Great Britain and France, a large number show views of U.S.A., Switzerland and The Holy Land with, less often, Canada, Turkey, Spain, Germany and Australia.

When collecting stanhopes it is important that the picture is reasonably clear but if the object is rare a collector will accept a slightly imperfect view. The number of pictures contained in any particular 'peep' varies enormously. The largest number the author has seen is sixteen and this was a view of Paris surrounded by fifteen Heads of State. The majority of 'peeps' have either six views or just a single view.

The needlework tools with stanhopes in Colour Plate 176 show some of the varieties collectors can find. The vegetable ivory tape-measure (six views 'Souvenir of the Isle de Wight') and the red stained parasol needlecase (six views 'Great Yarmouth') are the tools to be found most readily, however, it is rare to find an ivory parasol needlecase (single view 'La maison de conversation à Bade-Bade') with such an elaborate carved finial on the handle. The carved wooden walnut thimble holder (single view 'Ballaigues La Sapinière') and the bone fish needlecase (single view 'Le St. Sepulcre') are also examples often seen. However, the coquilla wax holder (single view 'Vue Du Jourdain'), coquilla fish needlecase

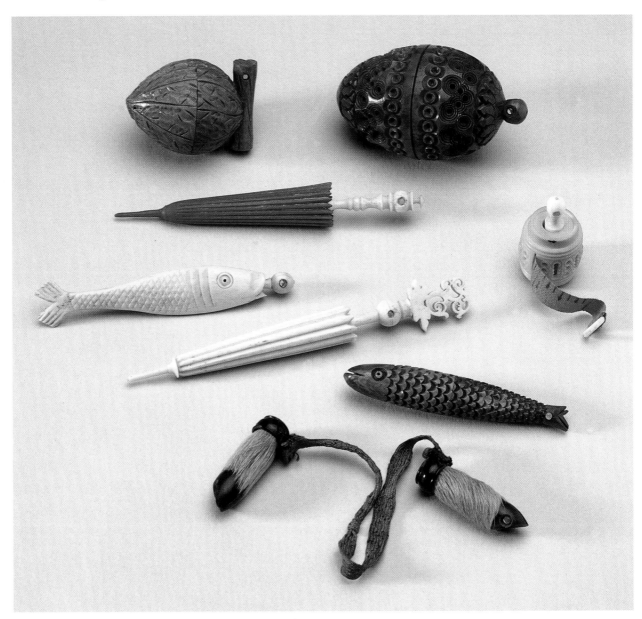

Colour Plate 176. A large range of needlework tools fitted with Stanhopes. Back to front:-wooden walnut thimble holder, coquilla wax holder, red stained parasol needlecase, bone fish needlecase, vegetable ivory tape-measure, ivory parasol needlecase, coquilla nut 'fish' needlecase and hoof knitting needle guards. Mid Victorian. Length of bone fish needlecase 3¾in. (9.6cm.)

(single view 'Resurrection of Jesus Christ') and the hoof knitting needle guards (six views 'A Memory of Bridlington Quay') are quite rare.

A tremendous number of needlework tools that are fitted with stanhopes are made from vegetable ivory and a lesser number from coquilla nut. Vegetable ivory is the inside nut of the corozo palm – the endosperm from the palm *Phytelephas Macrocarpa*. This palm has always been considered a native from South America but recent evidence shows that at least a small amount came from Africa. A large variety of needlework tools were made from vegetable ivory as it lent itself beautifully to lathe turning. Craftsmen were not limited by the size of the nut but cleverly fashioned large articles that on close inspection prove to be made in sections that screw together. A new nut from this palm is a lovely ivory colour

Colour Plate 177. Vegetable ivory was an ideal material for the construction of this large range of needlework tools. Back row:- basket pincushion, standing bodkin case, standing needlecase, thread holder, tape-measure. Middle row:- shell-shaped pincushion, urn-shaped pincushion, acorn-shaped sewing set, egg-shaped wax holder. Front row:- emery cushion, combination reel/pincushion, needlecase, waxer. c.1870 - 1880. Height of bodkin case 3½in. (9cm.)

that mellows with age to a variety of honey shades. The variety of needlework tools made from vegetable ivory is shown in Colour Plate 177. Pincushions were made in the shape of a basket, urn or shell, another has an attached reel for thread and the smallest with purple velvet ends is filled with emery. The standing bodkin case and standing needlecase have each been made from three pieces of vegetable ivory that screw together as has the smaller needlecase. Some shapes are obviously made from two sections of vegetable ivory that screw together, this being the case with the beehive-shaped thread holder, egg-shaped waxer and acorn-shaped holder for needles, threads and thimble. Even the two sides of the disc-shaped waxer unscrew so that replacement wax can be inserted. The tape-measure has been fitted with a stanhope at the top of the spindle. Both the ring at the end of the tape and the spindle are made from bone, something that is quite usual.

The coquilla nut also came from a South American palm known commonly as the Piassava palm or technically as *Attalea Funifera*. This palm is grown primarily for its coarse brown fibre that is used in the making of ropes and brushes and the nut is of secondary importance. The outer shell of the coquilla nut is the only part used from the Piassava palm and this explains why articles made from coquilla

Colour Plate 178. Wax holders. Back:- both of these egg-shaped holders are made from coquilla nut, one has been fitted with a Stanhope. Front:- carved wooden lemon-shaped container for wax, two other wax holders — one of ivory the other vegetable ivory. c.1870 - 1880. Length of ivory egg 2¼in. (5.8cm.)

nut have a lathe turned exterior and are hollow inside. Some needlecases were made from coquilla nut – one in the shape of a fish fitted with a stanhope view is featured in Colour Plate 176, but the usual needlework tool found made from this material are the overwhelming number of egg-shaped wax holders. Two of these coquilla nut wax holders are shown in Colour Plate 178, both their colours and lathe turning being quite distinctive, and one has been fitted with a stanhope view. Two other egg-shaped lathe turned wax holders are also shown in this colour plate, one of ivory, the other vegetable ivory. The carved wooden lemon was another container used to hold wax.

When John Taylor wrote the following lines in the seventeenth century, a needle was a treasured possession –

'To all dispersed sorts of Arts and Trades,
I writ the needles prayse (that never fades),
So long as children shall be got or borne,
So long as garments shall be made or worne,
Yea till the world be quite dissolv'd and past;
So long at least, the Needles use shall last.'

A century later a needle-making industry was flourishing at Redditch in England; in fact, there were about 400 needle makers in the area.

This industry continued to flourish for the next century and by the middle of the nineteenth century the leading needle producers were becoming extremely competitive. No doubt various ideas to promote a particular brand of needle were tried but the 'novelty' that outshone all others were the various needlecases made of brass.

At this time, the leading manufacturers of needles were J.W. Lewis, W. Avery & Son, H. Milward & Son and Able Morall. What is interesting, however, is that, although all these needle makers produced brass needlecases, collectors today generally refer to all brass needlecases as 'Averys'. William Avery, the son of a needle manufacturer, was born in 1832. He had many diverse interests, one of which was photography which he put to good use when he travelled throughout

Colour Plate 179. Brass needlecases. Back:- butterfly made by William Avery in 1871, Beatrice made by William Lewis in 1867. Front:- quadruple golden casket made by William Avery in 1868, the fan made by H. Milward. c.1870. Width of butterfly 5in. (12.7cm.)

Europe with his wife. It is possible that Avery's hobby of photography later led to the invention of the figural needlecases.

William Avery was a very ambitious man looking for avenues to develop his business. In 1867 he produced metal counter boxes to replace wooden boxes previously used to display packets of needles. What is interesting, is that in the same year a competitor, a Birmingham jewellery manufacturer named William Lewis, patented and produced the first brass needlecase called the 'Beatrice' (Colour Plate 179). The Beatrice was like a miniature folding screen with either four or six sections to hold packets of needles of different sizes. The arrival of the Beatrice onto the market must have given William Avery the impetus to invent his first brass needlecase – 'The Golden Casket'. This needlecase was a simple decorated brass covering to hold a single packet of needles. The following year (1868) a most innovative brass needlecase was produced by Avery. This was named the Quadruple Golden Needlecase (Colour Plate 179) and patented jointly by William Avery and his machinist Albert Fenton. This needlecase was a

Colour Plate 180. Brass cotton reel stands. The brass posts, with either brass figures or ivory finials, pull up to allow reels of thread to be fitted. c.1870-1880. Height of left stand 18in. (45.8cm.)

rectangular box with four interior sections that could be raised by moving a lever, each section holding a different size needle packet. This quadruple needlecase proved to be so popular eventually twelve versions were produced, some by Avery's competitors.

From 1868 until the end of the 1870s a virtual flood of brass needlecases was produced, reaching a peak in 1872. It would appear that each design was created to 'out-do' the previous one. A great number of these variations were patented and we are indebted to the research of Estelle Horowitz and Ruth Mann (two American collectors) for a record of these varieties in their comprehensive book *Victorian Brass Needlecases*.

Brass needlecases can be divided into various sections – the flat varieties, the quadruples and the figurals. This last section is where we find the rarest varieties and the most innovative designs. People are often amazed to find out that the brass

Colour Plate 181. French gilt metal pincushions. Left:- 'La hotte' – a basket of the type worn by French grape pickers for the wine harvest. Right:- the lady's padded velvet skirt is a pincushion. c.1860. Height of lady 4½in. (11.5cm.)

Colour Plate 182. Miniature pole screen pincushion. The cushion around the circumference holds the pins. English. Early Victorian. Height 8½in. (21.6cm.)

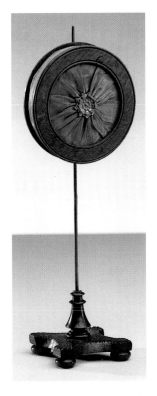

Butterfly Needlecase (Colour Plate 179) was made just to store packets of needles under its wings – the always popular butterfly was also used to decorate a box and a quadruple. The working drawings of the butterfly needlecase are works of art and have been reproduced in the book *Victorian Brass Needlecases*. A bee, a bird, a scallop shell and a hedgehog are just some more needlecases inspired by nature as are some of the lovely floral designs. Buildings, furniture, carts and baskets – all were produced in miniature in brass to hold packets of needles. Very occasionally a brass needlecase was produced that had a coloured cardboard interior and The Fan Needlecase (Colour Plate 179) has floral cardboard leaves to hold packets of needles.

The vast majority of brass needlecases were made between 1867 and 1876 but towards the end of the nineteenth century a few brass needlecases were produced as Royal Commemoratives, the most common being a quadruple produced for Queen Victoria's Jubilee in 1897 and this was probably made as a last effort to revive interest in these novelties but changing times brought an end to this innovation.

Stands to hold reels of thread were fashioned from wood or metal (Colour Plate 180). The more ornate had figures decorating the base, top and posts while the more functional had a pincushion fitted above the reels of thread. Each reel could be replaced by lifting up the posts by their finials.

The two velvet and gilt pincushions (Colour Plate 181) are delightful French examples and would have been proudly displayed by any lady in her salon. The gilt metal basket pincushion is a copy in miniature of the basket worn on the French grape-picker's back when picking grapes for the wine harvest. The lady's velvet skirt is padded so it can be used as a pincushion.

The miniature pole-screen pincushion (Colour Plate 182) is early Victorian and typically English. The pins were pushed into the circumference of the pink cushion that fits into the frame of the screen.

Colour Plate 183. Filigree base metal chatelaine with five original matching appendages that are all for needlework. They are a pincushion, thimble holder, scissors' scabbard (with scissors), needlecase and tape-measure. c.1880. Length 13½in. (34.4cm.)

Colour Plate 184. Rosewood table embroidery frame with ivory mounts, finials and feet. c.1840. Length 14½in. (36.8cm.)

Ladies' magazines during the late Victorian era were full of advertisements for chatelaines for needlework and they reached a peak in 1888. Most of the chatelaines advertised have five appendages and one of these is usually a non-needlework piece i.e. a notebook. However, the chatelaine (Colour Plate 183) has five appendages that are all needlework tools :- a disc pincushion, a thimble holder, a scabbard for a pair of scissors, a needlecase and a tape-measure with the original blue silk tape. These base metal chatelaines were always advertised and sold complete with appendages of a matching pattern.

Most needlewomen use some form of embroidery frame. It may be just a simple round double wooden ring or a large heavy wooden floor frame that is not portable and keeps the embroiderer sitting in the same place when working. However, table models were popular and the rosewood embroidery frame (Colour Plate 184) that has an adjustable frame that pivots on two pillars, is a fine example. Ivory mounts, finials and feet give this frame a finishing touch. A very similar embroidery frame (Plate 10) is illustrated in *The Handbook of Needlework* by Miss Lambert published in 1843 and she states that 'Both standing and table frames are frequently made of the finest and most expensive woods, when they may be rendered most elegant pieces of furniture for the boudoir.'

Plate 10. Sketch of embroidery frame showing embroidery in place.

Colour Plate 187. Needlework tools decorated with a complete covering of beads. Top and anti-clockwise:- egg-shaped thimble holder, pincushion, two cylindrical needlecases and a leg-shaped needlecase. Also shown is a miser's purse, each end finely knitted with beads. Early to mid Victorian. Length of leg needlecase 2¾in. (7cm.)

Colour Plate 185. (Opposite). Three hand-made fabric pincushions:- one with a hand painted cat, the popular jockey's cap and one a delightful silk pansy. Also shown a mourning combination needlecase and pincushion initialled on one side SW and dated 1849 on the other. Mid 19th century. Diameter of cat pincushion 2½in. (6.4cm.)

Chapter Ten

Victorian Crafts

There was nothing a Victorian Lady enjoyed more than attending her sewing circle regardless of whether it was held in an elegant drawing room or in a village hall. The attraction was not just the plying of a needle. It was the time to exchange patterns, examine new sewing requisites and, of course, there were the inevitable 'tales to be told'. This was the time that a recently purchased pincushion or needlecase was produced and proudly displayed. It was also the time when a hand-made pincushion or needlebook was critically scrutinised by those assembled, the creator sometimes waiting with trepidation for the comments of her peers. A great number of these hand-made pincushions and needlebooks have survived – the majority of an extremely high standard of workmanship. Were tiny stitches, evenly spaced, achieved by all Victorian ladies or is it more likely that pieces of inferior workmanship were not treasured and kept?

Disc pinwheels, identical to those made by school children in the mid twentieth century, date back to the early Victorian era. One pinwheel illustrated (Colour Plate 185) has been joined by ribbon to a second disc with leaves of flannel fitted between the two discs to form a needlebook. Doubtless this has been made to commemorate a death and mourning needlework tools are extremely rare. Black silk has been used for the covering fabric, black silk ribbon for the ties and even the leaves are made from black flannel. On one side the initials SW have been embroidered in gold thread and the year, 1849, has been worked on the other side.

Colour Plate 186. Berlin woolwork slippers that have been embroidered from a graphed design similar to the example in Plate 11. As these slippers were never made up they have been preserved for future generations. Early Victorian. Length 14in. (35.7cm.)

Another disc pinwheel has been made from black silk and a cat hand-painted on one side. The same disc idea has been used for the pansy pincushion, in this case two shaped discs producing a delightful effect. Pansies were an extremely popular motif during the Victorian era as they portrayed the idea of 'thoughts' or 'thinking of you'. Another pincushion featured in this group (Colour Plate 185) is in the form of a jockey's cap and this is probably the hand-made pincushion most likely to be found by collectors today. Magazines during the Victorian era were full of patterns for pincushions and needlebooks and the directions to make a jockey's cap far outnumber any other style.

During the first half of the Victorian era the most popular form of embroidery was Berlin woolwork. This embroidery was worked on square-meshed canvas with worsted wools mainly in tent and cross-stitch. The stitches were copied from patterns printed on squared paper exactly as counted cross-stitch is now worked.

Patterns for this form of embroidery varied enormously and were published in Berlin about 1804 by the firm of A. Philipson and later by another Berlin publisher, L.W. Wittich. These patterns were imported into England early in the nineteenth century by Ackermann (well known for his *Repository of Arts 1809-1828*) and later by Mr. Wilks the owner of a needlework shop in Regent Street, London. There is an advertisement in *The Illustrated London News*, Dec. 14th, 1844 for Wilks' Warehouse as follows:-

A superb assortment of wools of all kinds - plain,
chine and shaded, including the four thread Berlin wool
… the largest and best assorted stock in the Kingdom.
Berlin patterns and every other Article … used in
Decorative Needlework.

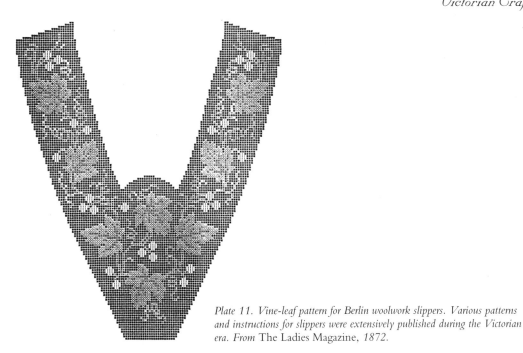

Plate 11. Vine-leaf pattern for Berlin woolwork slippers. Various patterns and instructions for slippers were extensively published during the Victorian era. From The Ladies Magazine, *1872.*

At the time of Mr. Wilks' advertisement over 14,000 different designs for Berlin woolwork had been published and cover every conceivable subject. As previously mentioned, these patterns were copied by the makers of Tunbridge ware (Colour Plate 119) and often an embroidery pattern can be matched to this intricate craft as can be seen in the Berlin woolwork sampler in Colour Plate 121. To give greater effect sometimes the pile was cut – this is often seen in embroideries of dogs – and beads were used to highlight, for example, the handle of a sword.

Enormous numbers of Berlin woolwork slippers must have been embroidered judging by the number of incomplete examples seen today. The pair featured in Colour Plate 186 have at least been completely embroidered and possibly if they had been 'made-up' and worn would not have survived to be preserved by late twentieth century collectors. The vine-leaf pattern for Berlin woolwork slippers (Plate 11) was published in 1872 in *The Ladies Magazine* and is just one of dozens of patterns for slippers that can be found in magazines of that era.

Berlin woolwork went out of fashion during the third quarter of the nineteenth century and although examples used for covering chairs, footstools and fire screens have often deteriorated from constant use, framed pictures are to be found in vast numbers.

Beads were used extensively to decorate hand-made needlework tools or were used on their own to form the complete covering. The three needlecases, 'egg' thimble case and pincushion in Colour Plate 187 have been made with a complete covering of beads. The cylindrical needlecase, the needlecase shaped as a leg and the egg-shaped thimble holder have been made in the same manner. An ivory, bone or wooden frame was first made and then the beads were formed as a covering onto the shape. Both of these needlecases pull open at the centre and needles fit into a hollow interior. The thimble holder unscrews at the centre. The pincushion has a bead-work cover that fits over a padded cushion – both sides being identical. Sometimes these bead-work pincushions were fitted with grains of emery. Also included in this colour plate is a miser's purse, the central section crocheted and the ends finely knitted forming a complete covering of beads. Miser's purses originated in the Georgian era but retained their popularity with patterns still being published in the 1870s.

Colour Plate 188. Hand-made needlework tools decorated with beads. Back:- pink silk slipper with a flannel inner-sole for needles – a thimble fits into the toe – Early Victorian; pair of slippers – one a pincushion and the other a needlebook. c.1870. Front:- two pincushions typical of the early Victorian era; left example decorated with beads; right example knitted with beads forming the date for William IV but this style extended into the reign of Queen Victoria. Length of slipper 3¼in. (8.3cm.)

Another group of needlework tools (Colour Plate 188) have had beads added for decoration. The pincushion dated 1834 has been made in three sections. Each side has been knitted with silk that has already had beads threaded along its length. The pattern is then achieved by placing the beads between stitches as required. The two sides have been joined around the circumference with a silk ribbon, the interior filled with padding. The disc pinwheel has been made from two pieces of silk material, one of which has previously been embroidered with beads. The tiny pink slipper appears to be at least early Victorian as the beads are so fine but care must be taken when dating any hand-made item. It is quite possible that silk material and beads were used that had been handed down from mother to daughter and twenty years later thought to be ideal for a needlework fancy. The little slipper was designed to hold a thimble in the toe and a piece of flannel fitted along the length of the sole was ideal for needles. Sometimes small pins were inserted around the

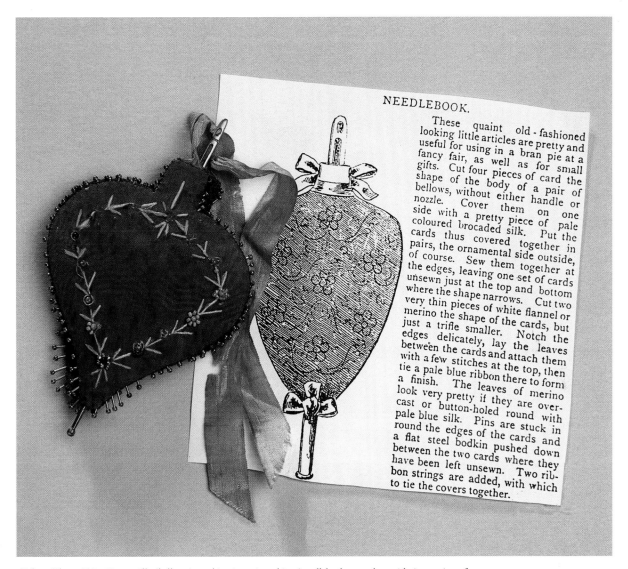

NEEDLEBOOK.

These quaint old-fashioned looking little articles are pretty and useful for using in a bran pie at a fancy fair, as well as for small gifts. Cut four pieces of card the shape of the body of a pair of bellows, without either handle or nozzle. Cover them on one side with a pretty piece of pale coloured brocaded silk. Put the cards thus covered together in pairs, the ornamental side outside, of course. Sew them together at the edges, leaving one set of cards unsewn just at the top and bottom where the shape narrows. Cut two very thin pieces of white flannel or merino the shape of the cards, but just a trifle smaller. Notch the edges delicately, lay the leaves between the cards and attach them with a few stitches at the top, then tie a pale blue ribbon there to form a finish. The leaves of merino look very pretty if they are overcast or button-holed round with pale blue silk. Pins are stuck in round the edges of the cards and a flat steel bodkin pushed down between the two cards where they have been left unsewn. Two ribbon strings are added, with which to tie the covers together.

Colour Plate 189. Green silk 'bellows' combination pincushion/needlebook, together with instructions from Mrs. Leach's Fancy Work Basket (published 1886/7) for the construction of a similar needlebook. Length 2¾in. (7cm.)

edge of the sole of the slipper. At the right rear of this colour plate is a pair of slippers joined together with a bone silk bow. One of these slippers is a pincushion - the pins fitting into the base, the other opens up and has flannel leaves inside so that it forms a needlebook. Beads have been used to decorate the edges and the sides of each slipper. When comparing the pale pink slipper and the larger bright pink pair, it is obvious that the tiny slipper is from a far earlier period of time and the larger slippers would date from the later Victorian era.

It is often possible to compare hand-made needlebooks and pincushions to published patterns and this does often give an indication of the date of their origin. The combination pincushion/needlebook illustrated in Colour Plate 189 aptly illustrates this point. Although not an identical shape, the 'bellows' hand-made green silk example could have been made by following the instructions shown in the same colour plate which were published numerous times over a long period of time – these instructions are from *Mrs. Leach's Fancy Work Basket* published 1886/7.

Colour Plate 190. Exquisite ribbon embroidery has been used to decorate this needlebook and two pincushions. Beads and wool embroidery have also been used to decorate the large needlebook. These are truly embroidered works of art. Early Victorian. Length of needlebook 3½in. (9cm.)

Ribbon-work creates a most delightful decoration on pincushions and needle-books. The two disc pinwheels (Colour Plate 190) have been embroidered in this manner and the needlebook in the same illustration has had beads and wool embroidery added to the two ribbon-work flowers to achieve an exquisite example of fine needlework. Again, it is very hard to date these examples, but it is thought they date from early in the Victorian era.

Ribbon-work has been used to delightful effect on the two lids of the bonbonnière box. This box is French and similar paper to the lining and the gold trim is seen on boxes dating from the middle of the nineteenth century (Colour Plate 191).

A gauze envelope to hold netting tools has been embroidered with fine half cross-stitch now known as petit point (Colour Plate 192). Although all the seams have been sewn by hand and the blue silk appears to be mid Victorian, there is no way that such a hand-made item can be accurately dated. One should just enjoy the ingenuity and workmanship.

Colour Plate 191. Bonbonnière box with lids delightfully decorated with ribbon embroidery. French. Mid 19th century. Width 7½in. (19.1cm.)

Colour Plate 192. Gauze envelope with petit point embroidery made to hold tools for netting. It is extremely difficult to date such hand-made items but it appears to be mid Victorian. Length 8in. (20.3cm.)

Knitting is one of the oldest crafts and remains of knitted clothing have been found in Coptic tombs dating from the fourth and fifth centuries. It is thought that originally the needles used had hooked ends but no proof has been discovered to verify this idea. However, it is known that by the fourteenth century straight needles were used and a painting 'The Visit of the Angels' by the Master Bertram c.1390 shows the Madonna picking up the stitches on four needles around the neck of a garment in exactly the same manner as any knitter would use today. Sheep's wool brought great prosperity to England and warmth to the majority of the population. It is said that the wealth achieved by the production of wool in England resulted in the tremendous number of magnificent churches that abound. Equally as important was the availability of wool for knitting and children learnt to knit almost as soon as they could hold needles. Most families relied for warmth on the clothing they could produce for themselves and consequently speed in knitting was of the utmost importance.

A knitting sheath was devised to be worn tucked into the belt on the right hip. The knitting needle (that was only about nine inches in length and had no knob at one end) slid into a hole at the protruding end of the sheath and the weight of the knitting was supported in this manner. The fingers of the right hand were then free to manipulate the stitches at the points of the needles and with practice great speed could be achieved. Scandinavians knit with very long needles, the ends of which are held firmly under the arm-pits. This is exactly the same principle as knitting with a knitting sheath.

Although knitting sheaths date back to the seventeenth century, the majority are of Victorian origin. The earliest known knitting sheath is dated 1615 and Edward Pinto knew of only eight dated seventeenth century sheaths in existence. The collection (Colour Plate 193) date from the mid eighteenth to the mid nineteenth centuries. From left to right the chip carved example is dated 1752 and initialled R H A B and is most likely a love token. The second has been carved so that the central section resembles a bridge and a wooden ball rolls around inside the end section that is known as an open lantern. This knitting sheath resembles a Welsh love spoon and it probably was a love token and came from Wales. The third example has an early wooden geometric inlay and at the other end, glass has been used in a frame to protect a paper-cut that has the hand-written inscription:-

Give God your heart
And he will Reward you. 1832

This sheath has a diagonal groove to accommodate an apron string. The fourth example is typical of knitting sheaths from the Branscombe area and the fish is quite unique and came from the W. J. Shepherd Collection. The most common style of knitting sheaths are those called goose wing knitting sheaths (the two examples on the right in Colour Plate 193) and this style is thought to have originated in the Yorkshire and Westmoreland Dales. One has been decorated with crossed incisions and the other has been punched with a triangular punch to create a quite pleasing effect.

Colour Plate 193. Wooden knitting sheaths. These useful implements were a necessity when speed was so essential to knitters. Early examples (from 1752) are included here with a range of Victorian sheaths. Length of fish 7in. (17.8cm.)

It is very easy for stitches to slip off a knitting needle that does not have a knob at one end. Knitters, of necessity, were very resourceful people and an ingenious device was created to solve this problem. Knitting needle guards were invented and these are two hollow caps or finials, one fitting over each end of a knitting needle and held tightly in place by the use of a piece of elastic, cord, ribbon or chain. Elastic would be the most satisfactory method of holding these two guards tightly in place but woven elastic was not in common use until the middle of the nineteenth century so cord, ribbon or chain would have been used prior to that date.

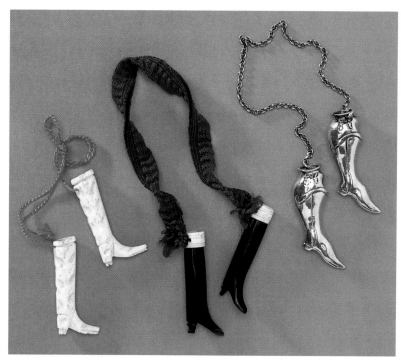

Colour Plate 194. Knitting needle guards in the shape of boots and made from bone, ebony and silver. The ebony boots have their original elastic and the silver pair are held in place by an adjustable silver chain. c.1840-1860. Length of bone boots 1½in.(3.9cm.)

Colour Plate 195. Knitting needle guards from left:- Dutch silver, English fretted ivory with original elastic and rosettes, miniature hoofs, carved ivory in the shape of a turbaned Indian gentleman. c.1840-1870. Length of silver example 2½in.(6.4cm.)

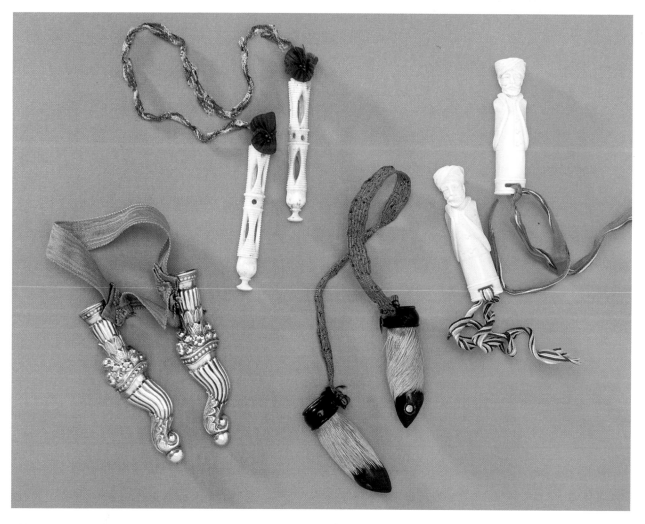

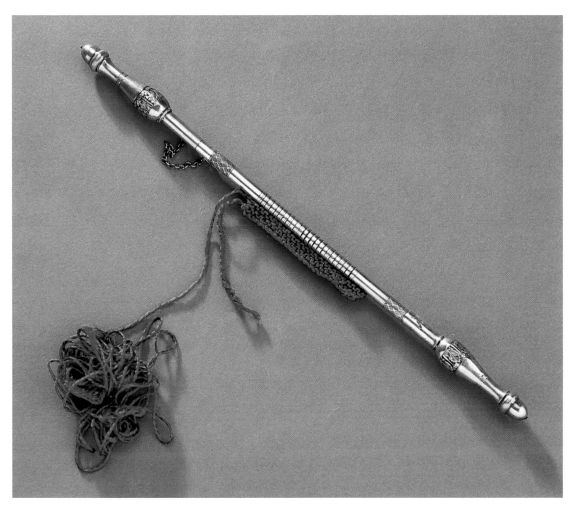

Colour Plate 196. Silver knitting needle guards that fit onto a matching central silver cylinder. A slit along one side of this cylinder allows the work in progress to protrude while the knitting needles and stitches are protected. Dutch. c.1870. Length 10½in. (26.7cm.)

The three knitting needle guards featured in Colour Plate 194 are each in the shape of a pair of boots but are made of three different materials – bone, ebony and silver. The ebony example still has its original elastic with the remains of a rosette where it is attached to the top of the boot. The silver boots are unmarked and similar examples are usually of Dutch origin.

The four knitting needle guards shown in Colour Plate 195 illustrate the range of varieties that were created. The silver pair again are unmarked but are most likely of Dutch origin while the fretted ivory pair are typically English and, although the rosettes are intact, the elastic is worn and perished. The third pair from the left have been made to resemble hooves and a stanhope view 'A Memory of Bridlington Quay' has been fitted into one hoof. The Indian gentlemen have been carved from ivory and a tremendous amount of detail can be seen in the facial features.

A more complex style of knitting needle guard is featured in Colour Plate 196 and although the two ends are the same as the more usual guards already featured, in this variety the two ends fit onto a cylindrical central section that has a slit along the length so that the knitting protrudes.

Silver knitting needle guards were also attached to a chatelaine waist clasp. The

Colour Plate 197. Silver
knitters' chatelaines. The
horizontal bar pulls open to hold
each end of the knitting needle as
illustrated. These chatelaines often
have a metal hook below the
waist clasp to hold the ball of
thread. c.1870. Length of anchor
4in. (10.2cm.)

examples shown in Colour Plate 197 pull open at the centre of the horizontal section and fit over the ends of the needle that holds the stitches. Quite often these knitters' chatelaines have a hook at the bottom of the waist clasp to hold a ball of thread. This hook can be clearly seen on the Berlin iron example featured in Colour Plate 198. This particular Berlin iron example is by far the rarest of all knitting needle guards ever seen by the author.

The Victorian era was a time of symbolism. The language of flowers, the unspoken message behind the way a fan was held, the colour of clothing worn, all had deep and meaningful significance. Victorian jewellery also followed suit and frequently one sees a piece of jewellery adorned by the letters 'F, H & C' representing the words Faith, Hope and Charity. More frequently one sees these words represented by the symbols – a Cross, an Anchor and a Heart. This symbolism carried over into Victorian embroidery where an abundance of overwhelming adornment was the norm. One example of this symbolic embroidery was the stitched Bristol board bookmarks and needlebooks that one still sees frequently. Victorian custom encouraged the giving of countless small gifts and even the most insignificant occasion would be marked by a token of love or remembrance. Birthdays, anniversaries, public and private occasions were all commemorated by keepsakes bestowed on friends and relatives and nothing was simpler than embroidering perforated board and making it into a bookmark or needlebook.

Bristol board is a stiffened paper that is punched with

Colour Plate 198. Rare Berlin iron knitters' chatelaine. The key pulls open at the centre to become needle guards. Suspended below the decorative waist clasp is a hook to hold a ball of thread. Mid 19th century. Length of key 4in. (10.2cm.)

Colour Plate 199. Embroidered Bristol board bookmarks. Although a great number of these bookmarks were of a religious nature and used for the family Bible, they were ideal gifts for all occasions. Embroidered leaves, a cross, a crown or an anchor are used symbolically instead of embroidering the actual word. Mid Victorian.

regularly spaced holes and it was used as a base for embroidery. It could be purchased in varying degrees of thickness and gauges of holes and was strong enough to hold stitches. Evenness of stitches was assured regardless of the talent of the embroiderer and, consequently, this craft was especially appealing to those less talented. The fact that so many of these frail items have survived is purely because of the overwhelming numbers that were produced.

The bookmarks featured in Colour Plate 199 are quite typical and the majority would have been used as markers in the Family Bible. An embroidered cross, an anchor or a crown are used symbolically instead of the embroidered words and embroidered leaves are used to complete the message 'Do not turn down the leaves but use me'. It would be fascinating to know the circumstances that inspired the inscription 'Remember the giver – Rebecca' or the simple 'Forget me not'.

Colour Plate 200. Three embroidered Bristol board needlebooks and a souvenir needlecase. The Bristol board in each of these examples has been decorated in a different manner to achieve a variety of decorative effects. Width of blue needlebook 2¼in. (5.8cm.)

The needlebooks in Colour Plate 200 have all been made from Bristol board but constructed in different manners. The cross has been formed by building up in layers cut pieces of board which contrast with the red satin that has been used as a base for the book. Flannel leaves have been fitted inside to hold the needles. The decorative effect has been achieved on the blue needlebook by carefully cutting away sections of the perforated board and a Victorian scrap has been added as a finishing touch. The needlecase with the word 'Souvenir' embroidered on the front in beads is also for needles. When the gold edge on the right is pulled out, one can see that it is actually an envelope and a packet of needles fits snugly inside.

Another Bristol board needlebook has been almost completely covered with bead embroidery – blue beads being used to form the words 'Forget Me Not'. This particular needlebook had been kept and passed down from generation to generation wrapped in an invitation that reads :-

Colour Plate 201. A Bristol board needlebook shown with graphed designs for this type of embroidery and a tiny embroidered slipper that has been made to hold needles and a thimble. The toe of this slipper has been embroidered as a sampler in a style similar to the graphed designs. Early Victorian. Length of slipper 3in. (7.7cm.)

Mr. and Mrs. Brine have the pleasure
to inform the ladies of Canterbury and its
vicinity that they have received their usual
Novelties for the Summer Season from the
Leading Houses of Fashion in Paris and
London, and that on Saturday next, May 3rd,
they will be prepared to show a Choice Variety
in Bonnets, Caps, Head Dresses, Flowers,
Mantillas, Embroideries, &c., &c., which they hope
will be favoured with an early inspection.
Waterloo House,
Canterbury, April 29th, 1856.

One can only speculate as to why this invitation was kept wrapped around the beaded needlebook.

Bristol board has also been used to construct the needlebook shown in Colour Plate 201 and the pages of graphed designs, also illustrated, are what a needlewoman followed when embroidering this perforated board. Also shown in this colour plate is a tiny slipper combination thimble holder and needlecase – the thimble fits into the toe and needles are kept in the flannel that has been used to line the sole of the slipper. This delightful little slipper has been embroidered as a sampler with the alphabet and numbers that correspond to those in the illustrated instruction sheet.

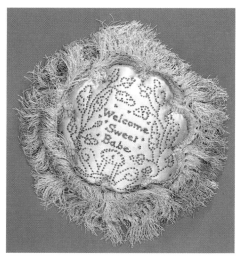

Colour Plate 202. Sampler book for 1854 that has an abundance of patterns for an embroiderer to copy. 3 x 2¼in. (7.7 x 5.8cm.)

Colour Plate 204. Layette pincushion. The heads of pins have been used to form flowers and the words 'Welcome Sweet Babe.' These pincushions are typical of Victorian sentimentality. Mid 19th century. Width without fringe 6in. (15.2cm.)

Young girls continued to embroider samplers right through the Victorian era and small books were published that were full of designs that could be followed. The sampler book for 1854 (Colour Plate 202) was produced by Groombridge and Sons, 5 Paternoster Row, London, and there are dozens of designs in the fold-out pages covering numerous scripts of the alphabet and numbers, as well as designs for flowers and animals and endless geometric patterns.

The Crystal Palace, erected in Hyde Park, London in 1851 was dismantled and re-erected in Sydenham, South London in 1854. The Exhibition that was housed in this building when it was originally built, remained as the major national event in England for decades and The Crystal Palace has been used as the major feature in a sampler (Colour Plate 203) completed by Elizabeth Jeffery of Chetnole in 1866. One wonders why Elizabeth featured The Crystal Palace – Exhibition 1851 – in her sampler, that was not completed until fifteen years later. Chetnole is a village in Dorset near Sherborne and it would have been quite a journey from there to London to visit The Crystal Palace. The verses embroidered on this sampler are worn and not easy to read but the first is:-

> Defer not till tomorrow to be wise
> Tomorrows sun on thee may never rise

The second verse is a Biblical text – Thessalonians IV:-

> Them also which sleep in Jesus
> will God bring with him.

Victorian sentiment was especially apparent with the making and giving of layette pincushions. These large pincushions were usually given prior to the birth of a baby which explains why most, if dated, only have the year. These large pincushions were made from cream satin with a silk fringe around the edge. The decoration and message on them was achieved by the placing of pins – the heads positioned so as to form letters, flowers and leaves. Although appearing to be an easy form of

Colour Plate 203. Sampler worked by Elizabeth Jeffery of Chetnole in 1866. The Crystal Palace is the major feature of this sampler even though it was embroidered fifteen years after the Great Exhibition was held in that building in 1851. 12 x 10in. (30.5 x 25.4cm.), excluding frame

decoration, 'pin-sticking' requires practice to achieve an artistic effect. The example in Colour Plate 204 has the message 'Welcome Sweet Babe' which with the message 'Welcome Little Stranger' are the most usual to be found. A pincushion in the Museum of Costume, Bath, England, inscribed 'May the Parent's wish be realised And the Babe prove a Blessing 1854' is a very down-to-earth message.

Although the art of tatting had been known for centuries it was about 1860 that this craft reached a peak of popularity. All crafts are cyclic and by perusing ladies' magazines it is possible to chart the rise and fall of the public's interest in a particular handcraft. An abundance of a particular needlework tool would have been necessary when a particular craft was at its peak of popularity and this does in some way help when determining the age of a particular tool. The method of tatting also changed during the nineteenth century and about the middle of the century an additional shuttle was used. A small crochet hook, known as a purling pin, was introduced to be used to pull through the loops to be joined and often a purling pin has a chain and finger ring so that the ring could be slid over the left

Colour Plate 205. Tunbridge ware tatting box with tatting and steel purling pin c.1840; ivory tatting shuttle c.1860. Length of box 4in. (10.2cm.)

Colour Plate 206. Mother-of-pearl egg-shaped tatting case lined with green silk and fitted with an ivory shuttle and gilt metal purling pin. The draw-string section inside the lid held small quantities of completed tatting. c.1860. Length 2½in. (6.4cm.)

Plate 12. H. Walker's catalogue, March, 1874, showing a tatting hook with gilt chain and ring and a tatting shuttle. The varieties of tatting shuttles are listed. It is also interesting to see listed at the bottom of this page 'Perforated Cards for Book Markers' (see Colour Plate 199).

thumb while tatting. A steel purling pin can be seen in Colour Plate 205 with a tatting box, ivory tatting shuttle, and an example of tatting. This tatting box is a rare Tunbridge example and was an ideal size to hold a shuttle, purling pin, thread and a small quantity of completed tatting. A gilt metal purling pin together with an ivory tatting shuttle can be seen as the fittings in the delightful little mother-of-pearl shell tatting case (Colour Plate 206). Small quantities of thread and completed tatting can be fitted inside the green drawstring silk pocket in the lid of this case.

In H. Walker's catalogue, dated March, 1874, a range of tatting accessories are advertised including shuttles made from bone, ivory and pearl shell (Plate 12). Also advertised is a steel Tatting Hook with gilt chain and ring – this manufacturer preferring the term 'tatting hook' to others who use the name 'purling pin'.

A purling pin and shuttle can be seen as part of the tools that fit into the hand-made drawstring work-case for Tatting (Plate 13). This pattern with instructions was featured in *The Ladies Magazine,* Nov., 1872 and is just one of many patterns and instructions published for fabric containers for embroidery requisites.

As the nineteenth century progressed the points or ends of tatting shuttles underwent a change. The points, or ends, were made without a gap and modern tatters now find it difficult to work with a shuttle unless it has 'tight points'. Towards the end of the 1800s, shuttles were made, especially in America, with a small hook or pick at one end and this was used instead of a purling pin.

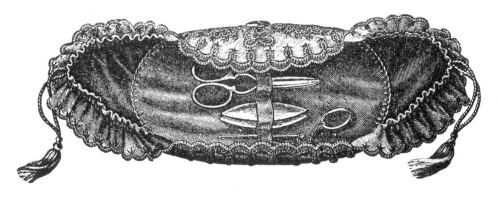

Plate 13. Illustration for work-case for tatting to be made of fine grey linen and blue silk, ornamented with grey tatting. A pair of scissors, a tatting shuttle and a purling pin are shown slotted into the base of this draw-string purse. From The Ladies Magazine, *1872.*

Colour Plate 207. Tatting shuttles. Back:- engraved sterling silver, engraved mother-of-pearl. Centre:- engraved mother-of-pearl, tortoiseshell inlaid with mother-of-pearl and silver wire. Front:- Canton carved ivory, polished horn. 19th century. Length of carved ivory 3¼in. (8.3cm.)

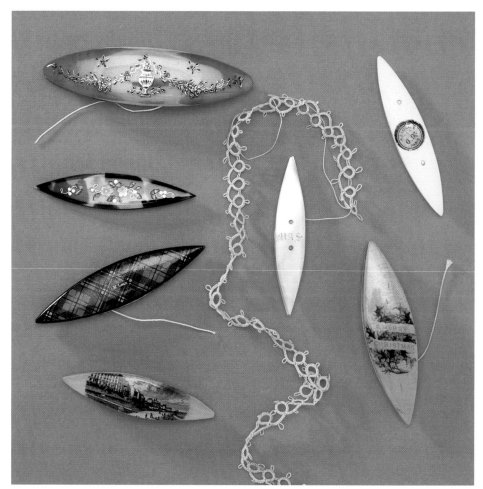

Colour Plate 208. Tatting shuttles. Left side:- tortoiseshell inlaid with a silver urn and garlands of flowers, tortoiseshell inlaid with mother-of-pearl and silver, tartan ware (McLean), Mauchline ware (Bridlington). Centre:- mother-of-pearl initialled M.A.S. with attached tatting. Right side:- ivory (with original retailer's label 'Au Louvre Paris'), sycamore wood decorated with holly and inscribed 'A Merry Christmas'. Length of mother-of-pearl shuttle 2½in. (6.4cm.)

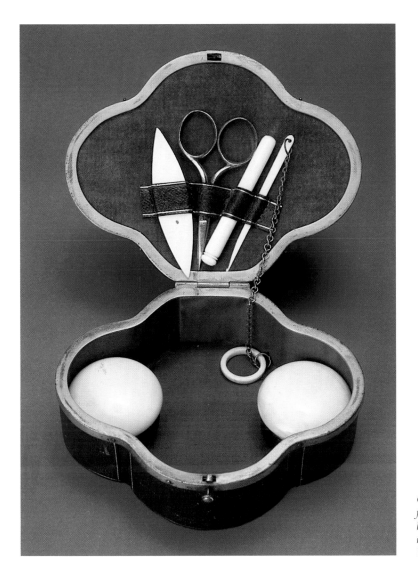

Colour Plate 209. Leather tatting box fitted with ivory boxes to hold beads. The lid is fitted with a shuttle, scissors, needlecase and purling pin. Late Victorian. Width 5in. (12.7cm.)

The tatting shuttles illustrated in Colour Plates 207 & 208 illustrate the amazing range of varieties of shuttles produced during the nineteenth century. The carved ivory shuttles made early in the century in Canton were rather impractical. They were gloriously carved but illustrate the lack of knowledge of their use by the craftsmen. The tortoiseshell with silver inlay, the sterling silver and the carved mother-of-pearl shuttles are all from early in the nineteenth century and their superb craftsmanship is far superior to the remaining shuttles featured in these colour plates. These remaining shuttles dating from about 1850 to 1880 are made of Mauchline ware, mother-of-pearl, Tartan ware, ivory, light horn, dark horn inlaid with silver and mother-of-pearl and even one shuttle of sycamore wood decorated with holly and inscribed 'A Merry Christmas'.

A tatting case dating from the late Victorian era is shown in Colour Plate 209. It is made of leather and the tatting shuttle and purling pin fit, with scissors and a needlecase, into sections inside the lid of the box. Two round ivory boxes in the base of the case were ideal to hold beads that were often incorporated into crafts. There was room in this case to hold small pieces of tatting. An abundance of sterling silver shuttles were in vogue at the beginning of the twentieth century and these will be discussed in Chapter 11.

Colour Plate 210. Wooden lace bobbins, left to right:- two bitted bobbins, chip carved lantern, chip carved, bitted with Kitty Fisher's eye bead on spangle, pewter bound inscribed 'Peter 1842', wire bound wood and bone, wood decorated with rings of beads. Early Victorian. Length of left bobbin, including spangle 4¾in. (12.1cm.)

It was inevitable that hand-made bobbin lace would, during the Victorian era, be replaced by laces that were made by machine. Queen Victoria tried to promote Honiton lace and used an extensive quantity to trim her wedding dress, but, by the end of her reign, machine-made lace was the only viable commercial proposition. The bobbins used by Victorian lace makers have now become collectors' items and with a resurgence of interest in this craft, most collectors are lace makers and antique lace bobbins have returned to their rightful place – on a lace pillow.

The lace bobbins used in various countries are quite different in appearance and traditional bobbins from the East Midlands of England are the only bobbins that have a ring of beads (called a spangle) at one end. They are also the only bobbins that usually have some form of decoration and consequently they have become overwhelmingly the most collectable lace bobbins. Bobbins were made of wood or bone or occasionally a combination of both, but usually, a bobbin made partly of wood and partly of bone means that two broken bobbins have been joined together to make one working example. This can be seen in the bobbin second from the right in Colour Plate 210. The wooden bobbins in this colour plate illustrate just a few of the decorative effects that were achieved by bobbin makers. From the left, the first two bobbins are called 'bitted bobbins' and the decoration

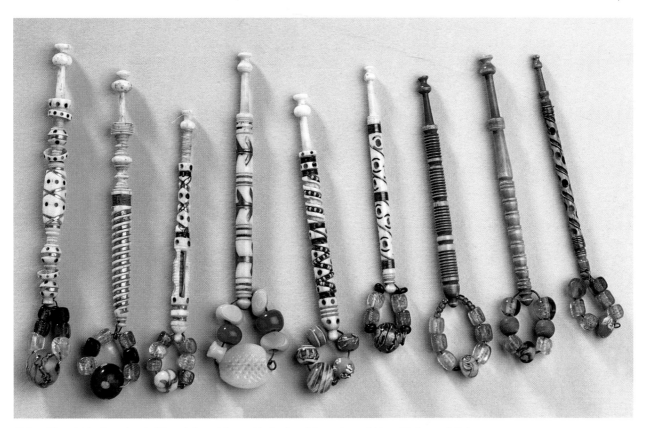

Colour Plate 211. Bone lace bobbins, left to right:- gold tinsel and loose rings, fairing, Mother and Babe, butterfly made by Bobbin Brown, wired and beaded, red dots and wired, stained red, stained mauve, green stained and wired. Early Victorian. Length of left bobbin, including spangle, 5in. (12.7cm.)

has been achieved by an inlay of a different coloured timber. The third and fourth bobbins have been 'chip carved', that is, whittled by hand. The first of these two is called a lantern bobbin and small beads are enclosed in the two hollowed compartments in the shank. The fifth bobbin is also a bitted bobbin, but in a more restrained form, with its most interesting feature being its bottom bead or a 'Kitty Fisher's eye' - a name derived from the popular Victorian actress. The sixth bobbin has rings of pewter and the largest ring in the centre is inscribed with indented dots 'Peter 1842'. The seventh bobbin, as already discussed, is half bone and half wood while the last wooden example has rings of tiny beads around its shank to give a most unusual decoration. The beads that form the spangles on lace bobbins are just as interesting as the bobbins themselves and these spangles frequently feature square cuts (usually red, pink, blue or clear glass beads that are square in shape) with Venetian glass beads on the bottom.

Bone bobbins were decorated in numerous ways and, just as hand-writing can identify a person, the manner in which a bobbin is made can sometimes identify the maker. The bobbin fourth on the left in Colour Plate 211 is a bobbin that is typical of one prodigious bobbin maker, William Brown of Cranfield, known as Bobbin Brown. This bobbin is called a 'butterfly' and has a distinctive pewter inlay that with some imagination looks like the wings of a butterfly when the bobbin is moved quickly across a lace pillow by a proficient lace maker. The bottom bead on this bobbin is called a 'sweetheart' or 'valentine' and as it is home-made, the heart shape is not as perfect as those that were produced commercially. The first two bobbins on the left of this colour plate are exquisite

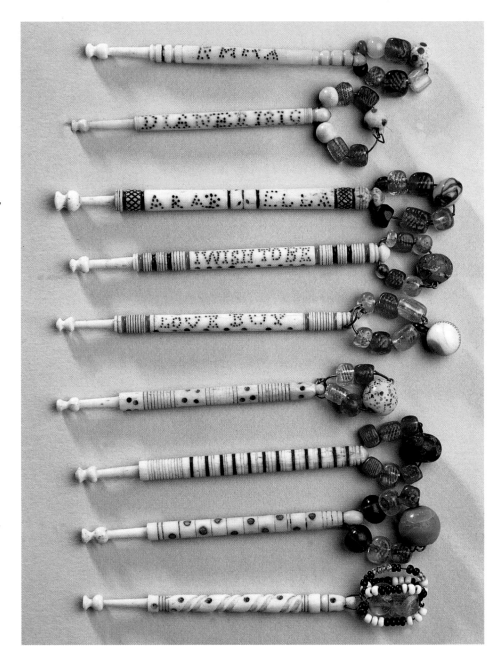

Colour Plate 212. Bone lace bobbins, top to bottom:- the first five are inscribed 'Emma', 'Dianer 1819', 'Arabella', 'I wish to be marred' and 'Love buy the ring'. Domino dots, tiger, leopard, decorated bobbin with a birdcage spangle. Early Victorian. Length of top bobbin, including spangle, 4½in. (11.5cm.)

works of art and were made by bobbin maker Haskins. He produced the most elaborate bone bobbins and the first of these two has three loose rings, coloured 'domino' dots and gold tinsel. The next bobbin, known as a 'fairing', has a spiral inlay of gold tinsel. The third bobbin is called a 'Mother and Babe' and a tiny green stained bobbin is enclosed in the hollow shank of this bobbin. The fourth bobbin, as previously discussed, was made by Bobbin Brown and the fifth bobbin has been spirally decorated with a wire threaded with tiny beads. The sixth bobbin has a binding of wire as well as large red dots and the three remaining examples show some of the colours used to stain bobbins.

Coloured dots were placed on bobbins to form letters and in this manner bobbins were inscribed with a name or a message. The bobbins in Colour Plate 212 are just a few examples of an endless variety – a named bobbin 'Emma', named and dated 'Dianer 1819', named with unusual decoration 'Arabella', a

Colour Plate 213. Honiton lace bobbins, left to right:- plain, aqua fortis, heart decoration, initialled HG and dated 1808, ebony initialled AF and dated 1822, heart decoration, fish decoration, pattern worn away with use, heavily incised with a bird and initials HT, Branscombe. Early 19th century. Average length 3¾in. (9.6cm.)

message 'I wish to be marred', and a message 'Love buy the ring'. Frequently the spelling on bobbins was incorrect as can be seen in the words 'Dianer' and 'marred'. The fourth bobbin from the bottom of this colour plate has a 'domino dot' decoration, an apt name as the dots are similar to those on dominoes. The next two bobbins are called a 'tiger' and a 'leopard' – their stripes and spots being achieved with pewter inlay. The bobbin at the bottom of this photo has domino dots and a spiral decoration, but it is the beads that are the important feature of this bobbin, as they form a birdcage spangle.

Often lace bobbins are incorrectly thought to have been made of ivory. This is almost always incorrect, as bobbin makers had no access to ivory whatsoever. The author has handled many thousands of lace bobbins over a period of twenty-five years and has only seen two bobbins that were definitely made of ivory. Both of these bobbins were of the 'Mother and Babe' variety and differed in appearance to bobbins made in the traditional lace making areas of England and it is possible that they were not made in that country.

The other English lace bobbins that have more recently become collectable are those used for making Honiton lace. These wooden bobbins do not have a spangle and the majority have no decoration and are similar to the bobbin first on the left of Colour Plate 213. The second bobbin on the left in this photo has been treated with aqua fortis to give a mottled effect to imitate tortoiseshell. As can be seen, various designs on these bobbins give a most pleasing effect with some in the form of geometric patterns and others in the shape of hearts, birds,

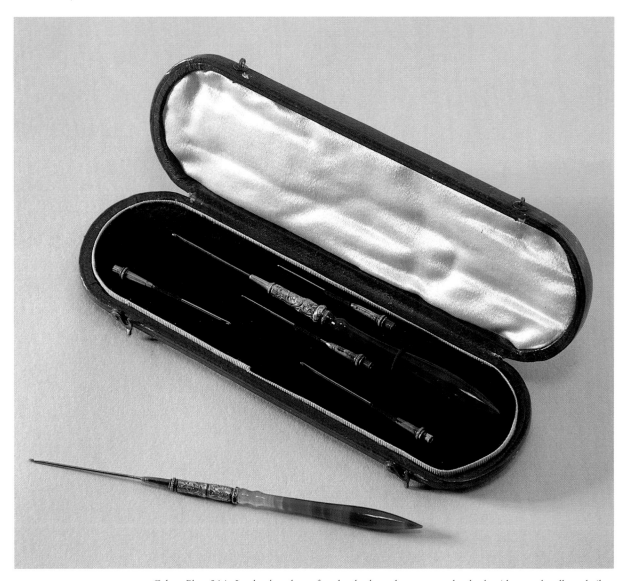

Colour Plate 214. Leather boxed set of crochet hooks and separate crochet hook with agate handle and silver mount. The boxed set has a choice of five different sized hooks that screw into an agate handle with a silver mount. One hook is shown attached to the agate handle. c.1860. Length 6¼in. (16cm.)

fish or trees. The bobbin, fourth from the left, has been initialled 'HG' and dated 1808, while the fifth is made of ebony, is initialled 'AF' and dated 1822. The bobbin on the right of this group has a decoration of coloured bands that is typical of bobbins used in the Branscombe area for making Honiton lace.

Some of the lace bobbins shown in the last four colour plates were made during the Georgian era, but they have been included with Victorian bobbins, as lace bobbins were so precious they were handed down by lace makers from generation to generation and would have been used during the Victorian era when the craft was fighting for survival. The twentieth century has seen the word 'craft' given a different connotation and the revival of interest in lace making has been as a pleasurable pastime and not as a necessity of life.

Although crocheting reached its peak of popularity at the end of the nineteenth and early in the twentieth century, it was a popular craft during most of the Victorian era. There is no doubt this craft was introduced into England by Mlle

Eleanore Riego de la Branchardière who fled France at the time of the Revolution. During the 1850s she produced a magazine called *The Needle* and published hundreds of patterns for crochet, many of these patterns still being used today.

Glorious boxed crochet sets were produced during the third quarter of the nineteenth century and many of these sets included a crochet hook with an agate handle (Colour Plate 214). The set illustrated has a selection of five different sized hooks that screw into the sterling silver mount above the agate handle – one hook is already attached to the handle. A similar unboxed agate handled crochet hook is shown in front of the boxed set.

Crochet hooks were also made with gold handles and the set in Colour Plate 215 has a choice of three different sized hooks to fit into the one handle. More utilitarian crochet hooks were made from brass and as the Edwardian era approached and crocheting became by far the most popular craft, crochet hooks were made from any suitable material.

Colour Plate 215. Gold handled crochet hook in a leather box with additional choice of two other sized crochet hooks. c.1860. Length 5¾in. (14.6cm.)

Colour Plate 216. An Edwardian lady's sewing basket, crochet and pattern book and her typical Edwardian sterling silver needlework tools. Left to right:- scissors, crochet hooks, stiletto, thimbles, thimble holders, chatelaine to hold a ball of thread and ribbon threaders. All the needlework tools are English and hallmarked for the Edwardian era. Width of basket 10½in. (26.7cm.)

Colour Plate 217. (Opposite). Leather boxed set of sterling silver handled scissors and sterling silver thimble. Birmingham 1904. Length 5in. (12.7cm.)

Chapter Eleven
The Edwardian Era

The Edwardian era was the era of sterling silver. Silver mining was on the increase, the price of silver decreased and a lady's dressing table was overloaded with sterling silver toiletry requisites. The use of sterling silver extended to the tools for embroidery that were now kept in a sewing basket that had replaced the sewing box. Sewing baskets were light and portable and more practical for the Edwardian lady who was more on the move. These baskets were lined with silk or satin and had pockets and divisions to hold various needlework tools. Colour Plate 216 shows a typical Edwardian lady's sewing basket, her needlework tools and an example of the major craft of that era, crocheting, and a pattern for a crocheted doily. The tools in this plate are a pair of sterling silver handled scissors, steel crochet hooks with either sterling silver or mother-of-pearl handles, steel stiletto with a sterling silver handle, sterling silver thimbles, sterling silver thimble cases, sterling silver ribbon threaders and a sterling silver ball (to hold a ball of thread) with a chatelaine waist clasp. All of these needlework tools have an English hallmark dating them from the Edwardian era.

Some sewing tools, of necessity, combine sterling silver with steel. This is to ensure the working section is strong enough for the work ahead. A stiletto will have a beautifully worked sterling silver handle but the awl section will be of steel

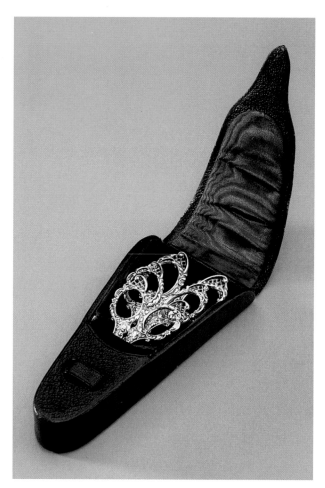

Colour Plate 218. Boxed set of three pairs of scissors in graduating sizes with decorative sterling silver handles. Birmingham 1902. Length of case 5¾in. (14.6cm.)

so it can be used to make holes in heavy fabric. It would be impossible to produce a working pair of scissors made entirely of sterling silver. Steel blades were fitted to handles of sterling silver that were made in many different styles. Even though sterling silver was combined with steel the overall impression when one looks at Edwardian embroidery tools is an abundance of silver.

Leather cases are often found that hold a pair of scissors with sterling silver handles and a sterling silver thimble (Colour Plate 217). Another leather case was designed to hold three pairs of scissors in graduating sizes (Colour Plate 218) and this set is hallmarked Birmingham 1902.

The major craft at this period of time was crocheting. Women's magazines were packed with patterns for crocheted edges, insertions and complete articles. There were also patterns for crocheted novelties and vast numbers were made to be sold at the local church fête or bazaar. Crocheting during the Edwardian era was almost always worked with white thread. White crochet was combined with white linen to make cloths of all sizes with table napkins to match. Huckaback towels with wide crocheted ends graced every bathroom and antimacassars, to protect the back and arms of chairs, were evident in every drawing room. The heavy white linen nightdresses of the Victorian era gave way to lighter versions that often had a crocheted bodice. Bedrooms were a sea of white with a bedspread of fine linen with crocheted insertions, pillow slips and sometimes pillows to match. It is not surprising that so much Edwardian crocheted household linen has survived when one realises that issue after issue of such popular magazines as *Needlecraft* were entirely devoted to promoting this craft. Bone crochet hooks were sold in vast numbers as were hooks of steel with mother-of-pearl handles. Stilettos, originally designed to pierce a hole in fabric for eyelet work or richleau embroidery, have come back into fashion in the 1990s. They are now used as an aid for wool embroidery and ribbon embroidery both of these crafts now being prominently featured in needlework magazines.

Vast numbers of holders for thimbles were made of sterling silver and the majority of these thimble holders, cases or buckets were designed as chatelaine appendages. The sterling silver thimble holder that is an appendage on the sterling silver chatelaine in Colour Plate 219 is one style frequently seen. The other appendages on this chatelaine that are for needlework are a pincushion (in the

Colour Plate 219. Sterling silver chatelaine (Birmingham 1902) with three appendages for needlework that are a disc-shaped pincushion, scissors' scabbard with scissors and thimble holder. The other two appendages are a notebook with its attached pencil and a glass and sterling silver perfume bottle. Length 12in. (30.5cm.)

shape of a disc) and a scissors' scabbard and scissors, the remaining items being a notebook with attached pencil and a perfume bottle. This English chatelaine is hallmarked for Birmingham 1902 and was made by Murdock & Jones. Sterling silver chatelaines reached one of many peaks of popularity during the early Edwardian years and glorious examples were advertised in ladies' magazines. The majority of these chatelaines had at least two appendages intended for needlework.

Colour Plate 220. American sterling silver needlework tools. Clockwise from rear:- embroidery ring, thimble holder (Unger Bros.), thimble (Simons' cupid), hem measure, glove darner (Webster Co.), winder (Webster Co.), strawberry waxer, strawberry emery and ebony darner with sterling silver handle. Early 20th century. Length of glove darner 4in. (10.2cm.)

A vast number of extremely high quality early twentiethth century sterling silver needlework tools are of American origin and a selection of these tools is shown in Colour Plate 220. One of these sterling silver tools, that was only made in America, is a hem measure. These delightful implements are extremely convenient to use and their popularity was such that Unger Bros., a prestigious American silver manufacturer, advertised sixteen different varieties in their 1904 catalogue. Sterling silver glove darners and sock darners of ebony with sterling silver handles are almost always of American manufacture and in an age when darning was an essential occupation and the wearing of gloves a compulsory social custom, darners were owned by every needlewoman. Of course, a simple mushroom-shaped wooden, or glass egg-shaped darner fulfilled exactly the same

Colour Plate 221. American sterling silver stiletto in the shape of a sword fish, a sterling silver tatting shuttle with fish motif and a set of three fish-shaped ribbon threaders. All of these needlework tools were made by the prestigious American silversmiths Simons Bros. Early 20th century. Length of stiletto 3½in. (9cm.)

purpose, but an elegant Edwardian lady preferred sterling silver. Strawberry emeries are as popular today as they were during the Edwardian era. A fabric cushion in the shape of a strawberry was filled with grains of emery and often the American version had silver leaves at the top as can be seen in this colour plate. A strawberry waxer, however, is extremely rare and the example illustrated next to the strawberry emery also has a silver leaf top and is of American origin. Also featured in this colour plate is a rare sterling silver embroidery ring of American origin, that fulfils exactly the same purpose as one made of wood, but no doubt this sterling silver embroidery ring would have been owned by a lady whose other needlework tools were also made from sterling silver. The sterling silver thimble case with its hinged lid and the sterling silver winder for silk thread are typical shapes favoured by American manufacturers and similar shapes were not produced by English silversmiths. The sterling silver thimble with a cupid pattern is American and was made by Simons Bros. although sterling silver thimbles with a cupid pattern were also made by English silversmiths.

Although most sterling silver ribbon threaders were manufactured in America, sets were also made in England and Scotland that were perfectly plain, whereas the majority of American sterling silver ribbon threaders are either engraved or have repoussé decoration. A large number of Edwardian under-garments were trimmed with lace insertion and an implement was needed to thread ribbon along the length of this insertion. The unusual ribbon threaders in Colour Plate 221 are in the shape of fish and are marked – 'patent July 11, 1905'. Also, in the same

Colour Plate 222. Spool knaves, left to right:- sterling silver hallmarked London 1902, silver plated, sterling silver in an ornate pattern hallmarked London 1906. The horizontal bar on these spool knaves unscrews so that a ball of thread can be put in place. Length of middle example 7½in. (19.1cm.)

colour plate, the fish on the tatting shuttle matches the ribbon threaders and the sword fish is an ideal shape to be utilised as a stiletto. All the implements in this colour plate were made by Simons Bros. A great number of sterling silver tatting shuttles were made of sterling silver in America, some having one end on one side extended to form a pick. Tatting did have a slight upsurge in interest early in the twentieth century and vast numbers of shuttles were sold, but it could in no way compete with the overwhelming popularity of crochet.

Edwardian ladies found it ideal to have their ball of thread hanging at their waist and a sterling silver thread ball with a chatelaine waist clasp has been shown in Colour Plate 216. However, the more usual implement for this purpose was a spool knave and although this implement dates back to the eighteenth century, there was a renewal of popularity late in the Victorian era. Spool knaves were made of silver plate or sterling silver, some hallmarked in Edinburgh but the majority were made by English silversmiths. The spool knave on the left of Colour Plate 222 is sterling silver and is hallmarked for London 1902. The middle example is silver plated and is a style that is frequently seen, while the right-hand sterling silver spool knave (London 1906) is of a more unusual elaborate design.

Edwardian sterling silver pincushions are the most common needlework tool to be found by any collector and they are usually of English origin. Every conceivable shape was fitted with a pincushion and shoes, slippers, wheelbarrows, animals and birds are just some of the varieties. It would be hard to find anyone who has not seen a sterling silver elephant or pig pincushion. The variety of animal and bird shapes used for pincushions is vast (Colour Plate 223). Some, for

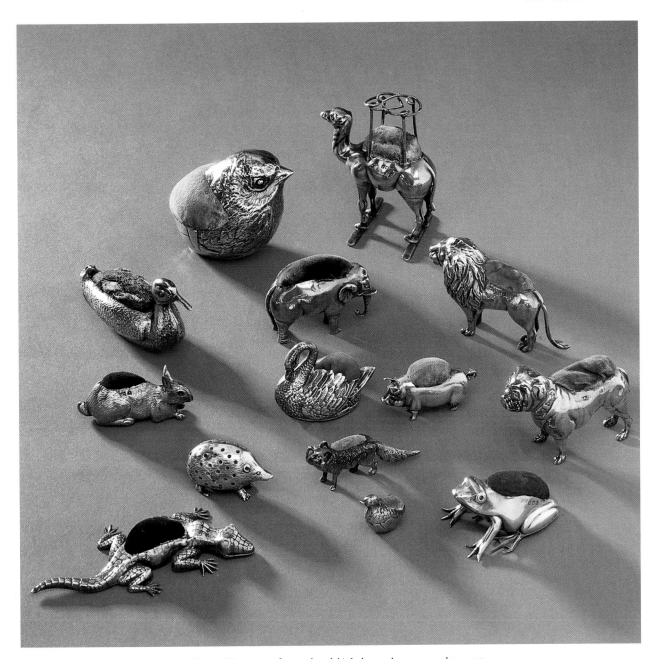

Colour Plate 223. Sterling silver pincushions. The range of animal and bird shapes that were used to create these delightful novelties is endless. These are just some of the varieties available and date from early in the 20th century. Length of lizard 4¼in. (10.9cm.)

example, chickens, pigs, elephants and frogs, were made in different sizes. Others, such as fox, pheasant, rabbit, lion, bulldog and St. Bernard dog are difficult to find but more frequently seen are camels, lizards, porcupines, swans and ducks. It is interesting to study the makers of these novelties to determine if one silversmith specialised in one particular shape. Overall it appears that the majority of sterling silver animal pincushions were made by Adie & Lovekin Ltd. Most of the chicken pincushions of all sizes were made by Samson Mordan and often are marked with the Registration No. 475678 and hallmarked Chester 1907 or 1908. The porcupines, ducks, swans, pigs and elephants examined by the author have been made by different silversmiths but the lizards have all been made by Calmon &

Neate. Of course, small sterling silver items are sometimes stamped with a retailer's mark when they were made for a particular retailer under licence, which makes identifying the silversmith difficult.

The English Needle Cases shown in Colour Plate 224 were advertised early in the Edwardian era and by the number available for collectors today they must have been extremely popular. The needle case shown closed on the back left of this plate was originally purchased enclosed in the cardboard box that is on the back right of this plate. Three sides of this closed needle case have been decorated with prints of Edwardian beauties, while the fourth side has a machine embroidery of flowers and the words 'With my Love'. The lid has a gold paper horseshoe and the words 'Good Luck' making it a gift for all eventualities. At the front of this colour plate another needle case is shown open, clearly displaying the inside of this case when it is unfolded. The lid of the central compartment lifts up so that a thimble and/or tape-measure can be stored inside.

During the whole of the Edwardian era, leatherette boxes were sold fitted with

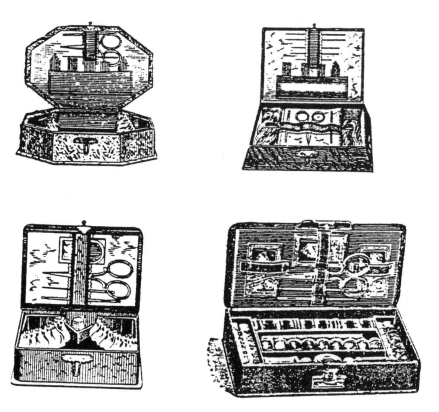

Plate 14. Four examples of leatherette boxes fitted with packets of needles, reels of thread, scissors and bodkins. These were advertised by Anthony Hordern & Sons, a large Australian Department store. From The Australian Home Journal, *1909.*

Colour Plate 224. English needle cases, one example shown closed with its original box. It has been decorated with a machine embroidery on one side and pictures of Edwardian beauties on the other three sides. A needle case is shown open so that the interior fittings can be seen. The padded lid on the central compartment lifts off and a thimble and/or a tape-measure was kept inside. Early 20th century. Height 4¼in. (11.5cm.)

packets of needles, reels of thread, a pair of steel scissors, thimble, and steel bodkins. These must have been extremely popular as the four examples (Plate 14) are just some of the varieties that were advertised in 1909 by Anthony Hordern & Sons, a large Australian department store.

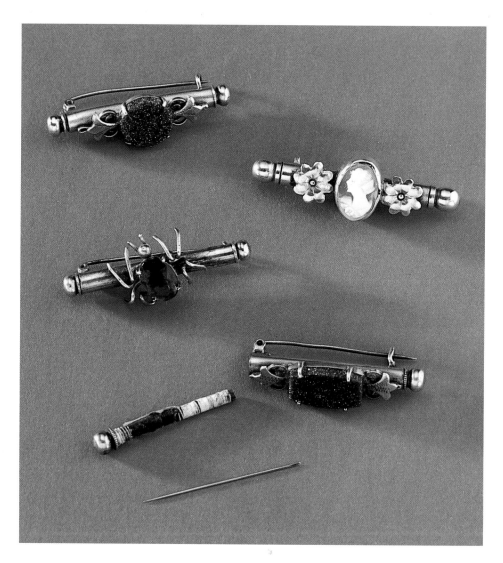

Colour Plate 225. Nanny brooches that were worn more as a badge of office than a practical sewing set. One end unscrews to reveal a cylinder that holds thread around the outside and a needle and pin inside the cylinder. The patent for this design was registered in 1895 but they were extensively used during the Edwardian era. The usual variety (back and front) were made of brass and decorated with brass leaves and a central synthetic goldstone. One of the other varieties shown has a decoration of a cameo while the other has a brass spider with a glass body. Length of nanny brooch with cameo 2in. (5.2cm.)

The Nanny Brooch (Colour Plate 225) is a delightful emergency sewing set that was patented in 1895 but was still very popular during the Edwardian era. It has to be the world's smallest sewing set and was worn more as a badge of office by a nanny than for serious sewing. The traditional version is made of brass and for a decorative effect has a central synthetic gold-stone (round, square or rectangular), with a brass leaf on either side. One end of the brooch unscrews and a cylinder inside pulls out to reveal the contents – thread around the outside of the cylinder and a needle and pin inside. Occasionally a brass spider with a coloured glass body was substituted for the usual gold-stone decoration. The nanny brooch, second from the top in this colour plate, is a different design to the traditional examples but one end unscrews in the same manner to reveal the normal contents. In this example the gold-stone is replaced by a poor quality cameo and other examples have been fitted with a cabochon moonstone or agate (grey or green).

Different periods of time produced their own typical style of needlework tool. Each is beautiful in its own way and a selection of Edwardian sterling silver tools complements any collection.

Glossary

Aide-memoire	Small notebook, with pencil, containing ivory or paper leaves.
Appendages	Various items suspended by chains from a chatelaine.
Averys	Brass needlecases made by William Avery and now a term used to include brass needlecases made by competitors.
Bodkin	Pointless thick needle with a large eye for threading ribbon or cord.
Chatelaine	From 1828 this word was used for a waist-hung fashion accessory. Now used retrospectively for waist-hung fashion accessories prior to 1828.
Clouté	From the French word meaning 'studded'. A decoration of steel nails seen on ivory or wooden implements.
Colifichets	Double-sided embroideries worked in silk on paper.
Compendium	A container fitted with a variety of implements.
Coquilla	The nut from the South American Piassava palm *(Attalea Funifera)*
Ear-spoon	A small implement - one end spoon shaped for removing wax from the ear.
Emery	Grains of a variety of corundum that is used as an abrasive and for polishing.
Equipage	Eighteenth century word for a waist-hung fashion accessory now called retrospectively a chatelaine. An etui is often the central appendage.
Etui	(Pronounced E-twee) A small container that holds a variety of implements and is often the central appendage of an eighteenth century equipage. The implements fit into an interior frame.
Lac	A resinous substance secreted by a scale insect *(Tachardia Lacca)*.

Mauchline	(Pronounced Mock-lin) Small wooden souvenir items produced in the Mauchline area of Scotland and decorated with a black and white transfer.
Nail	The measurement of two and a quarter inches seen on early tape-measures.
Parfilage/Drizzling	The unpicking of gold threads from a garment.
Pin-poppet	A small closed container fitted with a cushion for holding pins dating from the late 18th/early 19th century.
Piqué	A fine inlay of silver or gold decoration.
Pochette	An embroidered draw-string bag used to carry embroidery and implements.
Silk winders	Flat variously shaped discs that held silk thread.
Snowflakes	Very small exquisite silk winders with a decoration similar to a snowflake.
Spool Knave	A stirrup-shaped holder for thread that was worn at the waist.
Standing Compendium	A group of needlework tools (thimble, reel, needlecase etc.) that screw together to form a complete standing article.
Stanhope or Peep view	A miniature lens fitted with a miniature photograph at one end. Stanhopes were fitted into an endless variety of objects.
Stiletto	An awl for making holes in fabric for various forms of embroidery (e.g. eyelet work).
Straw-work	The decoration of an article with a fine marquetry of straw.
Stumpwork	Heavy padded raised embroidery popular in the mid 17th century.
Toys	An 18th century term for small articles, useful or ornamental and usually of an extravagant and costly nature. They were sold by Toy-sellers or Toymen.
Vegetable Ivory	The endosperm (inside nut) from the Corozo palm – *(Phytelephas Macrocarpa)*.
Yard Measure	A length of thirty-six inches and usually divided into a Quarter and Half Yard.

Bibliography

Books

Allemagne, Henry René d', *Decorative Antique Ironwork* (Catalogue of the Le Secq des Tournelles Museum of Rouen), Dover Publications Inc., New York, 1968

Andere, Mary, *Old Needlework Boxes and Tools,* David & Charles Ltd., England, 1971

Armstrong, Nancy, *Fans,* Souvenir Press Ltd., London, 1984

Baines, Patricia, *Spinning Wheels, Spinners and Spinning,* B.T. Batsford, England

Baker, John, *Mauchline Ware,* Shire Publications Ltd., England, 1985

Baker, Muriel, *Stumpwork, The Art of Raised Embroidery,* Charles Scribner's Sons, New York, U.S.A., 1978

Ball A. and Martin M., *The Price Guide to Baxter Prints,* The Antique Collectors' Club, Woodbridge, England, 1974

Benjamin, Susan, *English Enamel Boxes,* Orbis Pub. Ltd., London, 1978

Blum, Stella (ed.), *Ackermann's Costume Plates,* Dover Publications Inc., New York, 1978

Bly, John, *Discovering English Furniture,* Shire Publications Ltd., 1971

Boehn, Max von, *Modes & Manners - Ornaments,* J.M. Dent & Sons Ltd., London, 1929

Bond, Sylvia, *The History of Sewing Tools* (Part 6), Embroidery Vol 14 No. 4, 1963

Bradbury, Frederick, *Bradbury's Book of Hallmarks,* J.W. Northend Ltd., 1975

Brears, Peter C.D., *The Knitting Sheath,* Folk Life Volume 20, 1981-82

Caulfeild, S.F.A. & Saward, Blanche C., *The Dictionary of Needlework,* L. Upcott Gill, London, 1882

Cavallo, Adolph S., *Needlework,* Smithsonian Institution, U.S.A., 1979

Chancellor, Valerie E., *Medieval and Tudor Britain,* Penguin Books, England, 1967

Clabburn, Pamela, *The Needleworker's Dictionary*, Macmillan London Ltd., England, 1976

Clabburn, Pamela, *Samplers,* Shire Publications Ltd., England, 1977

Clifford, Anne, *Cut-Steel and Berlin Iron Jewellery,* Adams & Dart, England, 1971

Colby, Averil, *Samplers,* Shire Publications Ltd., England, 1964

Colby, Averil, *Pincushions,* B.T. Batsford Ltd., London, 1975

Crossman, Carl L., *The Decorative Arts of The China Trade,* Antique Collectors' Club, Woodbridge, England, 1991

Culme, John, *The Directory of Gold & Silversmiths, Jewellers & Allied Traders, 1838-1914,* Volumes I & II, Antique Collectors' Club, England, 1987

Davenport, Millia, *The Book of Costume,* Crown Publishers, New York, 1948

Delieb, Eric, *Investing in Silver,* Corgi Books, London, 1970

Dillmont, Thérèse de, *Encyclopedia of Needlework,* Mulhouse, France, 1924

Druitt, Silvia, *Antique Personal Possessions to Collect,* Peerage Books, London, 1986

Field, June, *Collecting Georgian & Victorian Crafts,* William Heinemann Ltd., London, 1973

Friend, Dorothy, *British Commemorative & Souvenir Thimbles,* Thimble Collectors International, U.S.A., 1987

Germain de Saint-Aubin, Charles, *Art of the Embroiderer,* Los Angeles County Museum of Art, U.S.A., 1983

Gill, Margaret A.V., *Tunbridge Ware,* Shire Publications Ltd., England

Gostelow, Mary (Consultant Editor) *The Complete Guide to Needlework,* Oxford University Press, England, 1982

Groves, Sylvia, *The History of Needlework Tools & Accessories,* Hamlyn Pub. Group Ltd., London, 1968

Hayden, Ruth, *Mrs Delany her life and her flowers,* British Museum Pub. Ltd., 1980

Hayman, Richard, *Church Misericords and Bench Ends,* Shire Publications Ltd., England, 1989

Holme, Randle, *The Academy of Armory or a Storehouse of Armory and Blazon,* Chester, 1688

Holmes, Edwin F., *Thimbles,* Gill and Macmillan Ltd., Dublin, 1976

Holmes, Edwin F., *A History of Thimbles,* Cornwall Books, London, 1985

Hopewell, Jeffery, *Pillow Lace and Bobbins,* Shire Publications Ltd., England, 1975

Horowitz, Estelle, and Mann, Ruth, *Victorian Brass Needlecases,* Needlework Treasures, U.S.A., 1990

Huetson, T.L., *Lace and Bobbins,* David & Charles, England, 1973

Huish, Marcus B., *Samplers and Tapestry Embroideries,* B.T. Batsford Ltd., London, 1990

Jackson, Sir Charles J., *English Goldsmiths & their Marks,* Dover Pub. Inc., New York, U.S.A., 1964

Johnson, Eleanor, *Needlework Tools,* Shire Publications Ltd., England, 1978

Johnson, Eleanor, *Fashion Accessories,* Shire Publications Ltd., England, 1980

Johnson, Eleanor, *Thimbles,* Shire Publications Ltd., England, 1982

Jull, Douglas, *Collecting Stanhopes,* D.S. Publications, 1988

King, Donald, *Samplers,* Victoria & Albert Museum, 1960

Klamkin, Marian, *The Collector's Book of Boxes,* David & Charles, England, 1972

Lambert, Miss, *The Hand-Book of Needlework,* John Murray, London, 1842

Leach, Mrs, *Mrs. Leach's Fancy Work Basket,* 1886/7

Lewis, Courtney C.T., *George Baxter The Picture Printer,* Sampson Low, Marston & Co. Ltd., London 1924

Lewis, Courtney C.T., *George Baxter Colour Printer His Life and Work,* Sampson Low, Marston & Co. Ltd., London, 1908

Lewis, Courtney C.T., *The Story of Picture Printing in England during the Nineteenth Century or Forty Years of Wood and Stone,* Sampson Low, Marston & Co. Ltd., London 1928

Lewis, Courtney C.T., *The Baxter Book,* Sampson Low, Marston & Co. Ltd., London, 1919

Marshall, F. & H., *Old English Embroidery,* 1894

McConnel, Bridget, *The Letts Guide to Collecting Thimbles,* Charles Letts & Co. Ltd., London, 1991

Morris, Barbara, *Victorian Embroidery,* Herbert Jenkins Ltd., London, 1962

Pelham Burn, Diane, *Thread Winders for Collectors,* Thimble Collectors International, U.S.A., 1989

Pinto, Edward H., *Treen and other Wooden Bygones,* Bell & Hyman, London, 1969

Pinto, Edward H. & Eva, R., *Tunbridge and Scottish Souvenir Woodware,* G. Bell & Sons, London, 1970

Proctor, Molly, *Needlework Tools and Accessories,* B.T. Batsford Ltd., London, 1990

Rogers, Gay Ann, *American Silver Thimbles,* Haggerston Press, London, 1989

Rogers, Gay Ann, *An Illustrated History of Needlework Tools,* John Murray Ltd., London, 1983

Springett, Christine & David, *Success to the Lace Pillow,* C. & D. Springett, 1981

Springett, Christine & David, *Spangles and Superstitions,* C. & D. Springett, 1987

Swain, Margaret H., *Historical Needlework,* Barrie & Jenkins, London, 1970

Tardy, *International Hallmarks on Silver,* 1985

Tardy, *Poinçons d'Or et de Platine,* 1988

Thomas, Mary, *Mary Thomas's Book of Knitting Patterns,* Dover Publications Inc., New York, 1972

Toller, Jane, *Prisoners-of-War Work 1756-1815,* The Golden Head Press, Cambridge, 1965

Warren, Mrs and Pullan, Mrs, *Treasures in Needlework,* Ward Lock, London, 1855

Whiting, Gertrude, *Old-Time Tools & Toys of Needlework,* Dover Publications Inc., New York, U.S.A., 1971

Wilson, Erica, *Erica Wilson's Embroidery Book,* Faber & Faber, London, 1977

Wilton, Countess of, *The Art of Needlework,* Henry Colburn, London, 1840

Wright, Thomas, *The Romance of the Lace Pillow,* Paul Minet, England, 1971

Yarwood, Doreen, *The Encyclopedia of World Costume,* Scribers, New York, U.S.A., 1978

Zalkin, Estelle, *Zalkin's Handbook of Thimbles and Sewing Implements,* Warman Pub. Co., U.S.A., 1988

Catalogues

Sears, Roebuck & Co. 1902

Treasures from India, The Clive Collection at Powis Castle

Use has been made of catalogues of specialist sales conducted by Christie's, South Kensington, and Phillips, Knowle and London.

Pattern Books and Trade Cards

Heal & Banks trade cards, Print Room, British Museum, London

Heal, Sir Ambrose, Samuel Pepys his Trade-Cards, *Connoisseur* Vol. 91, England, 1933

Trade Cards held at the Guildhall Library, London

Magazines

Ackermann's Repository, 1809-28

Ladies, The - A Journal of the Court, Fashion and Society, London, 1872-73

Lady's Magazine of Fashion Fancy Work & Fiction, The (Le Moniteur de la Mode), London, 1888-95

Lady's Own Paper, The, London, 1866-72

Lady's World, London, 1893-94

Needlecraft magazines, published by the Manchester School of Embroidery, all issues

Queen's Chronicle, The, London, 9 Sept., 1837

Queen's Own, The, London, 1841

Queen, The: The Lady's Newspaper and Court Chronicle, 1861-1912

Weldon's Practical Needlework – all issues

Magazine Articles

Swain, Margaret H., *Colifichets: the story of a search,* Embroidery – Summer 1967

Townsend, Gertrude, *Portrait by John Singleton Copley of a Lady 'Knotting',* Wadsworth Atheneum Bulletin, Hartford, Fall 1966

Index

Page numbers in **bold** refer to illustrations